MORE FOR YOUR MONEY GUIDE

# How to Go to College for Free

Linda Bowman

PROBUS PUBLISHING COMPANY
Chicago, Illinois

Library of Congress Cataloging in Publication Data Available.

ISBN 1-55738-219-0

Printed in the United States of America

BB

1 2 3 4 5 6 7 8 9 0

# TABLE OF CONTENTS

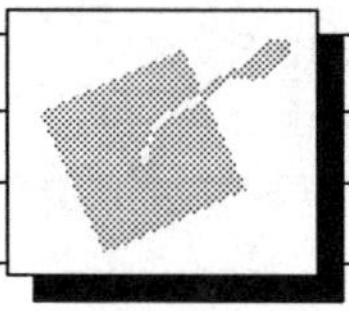

# INTRODUCTION

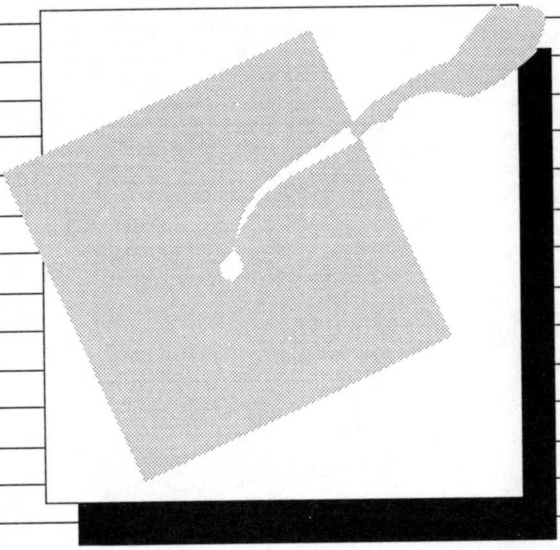

# INTRODUCTION

The largest single expenditure for a family today, other than purchasing a home, is paying for a college education. For families with two or three children, the amounts can become staggering. Add to this the probability that more than one child may be attending college at the same time, and the outlook becomes depressing.

To make matters worse, whereas paying for a family home can be stretched out over a period of 30 years, paying back college loans, if you can qualify for them, usually must be completed in a much shorter time, often five years.

College costs have continued to rise, and tuition hikes have been outpacing the inflation rate for the past several years. In the 1980s costs for attending a four year public institution were between $4,500 and $6,200 a year, and between $11,500 and $13,000 per year for a private institution. By the year 2000, the average cost for four years at a public school is expected to reach $40,000, and $100,000 or higher at private schools.

Since my children will be entering college in the mid-1990s and we are a two-income family who still struggle from year to year to make ends meet, I decided to look into alternative ways of financing my children's education. What I found is that there are many levels of financial aid available. I discovered that there are vast, often untapped, sources of free money for college—money that does not have to be paid back—to anyone—not ever. And it is 100 percent free when used for a student's college education!

Every year literally thousands of dollars of this free money for education goes unclaimed, just because students don't know how or where to ask for it. At best, the lucky few may find this "free money" by accident. My husband received a half-scholarship towards his law school tuition and fees only because he happened to be talking to a friendly professor who knew about a law school scholarship fund. In order to help you to avoid missing any of the thousands of dollars of free money, I have listed as many routes, sources, and possible paths to this money as I could find that are currently available.

Free money is available in three general forms: scholarships, grants, and through military programs which require service in the military following graduation.

The focus of this book is on these sources of free money. However, in the course of my research, I also discovered many other sources of funds, including loans, work-study programs, co-operative education, etc., and other creative money saving alternatives and programs for parents and students to help make the burden of four years at college a little easier.

Additionally, there are a few topics and rules one must become acquainted with if one is going to successfully play the "how-to-finance-the-kids'-education-and-keep-out-of-the-poorhouse-at-the-same-time" game. These are very important and include determining college costs, need analysis, application forms, financial aid packages, college aid "buzz" words, and sources of books and guides that can help educate you in choosing among the multitude of possibilities for student aid.

I hope this book will give you the determination and direction to investigate and take advantage of the avenues of free college money that are available now for you and your children. Good luck and get smart!

## INTERESTING FACTS AND FIGURES ABOUT ATTENDING COLLEGE

- More than $1 billion a year is awarded to qualified students by the armed forces.
- Approximately $30 billion in financial aid will be available for the 1990-91 school year.
- The largest number of academic scholarships are awarded by colleges. Approximately 86 percent of the four-year colleges in

**CHART 1**
**COLLEGE COST ESTIMATOR**

| | 1991 | 1994 | 1997 | 2000 | 2003 | 2006 |
|---|---|---|---|---|---|---|
| **When your child will begin college** | This year | in 3 years | in 6 years | in 9 years | in 12 years | in 15 years |
| **4-year public college will cost approximately** | $28,000 | $32,000 | $39,000 | $48,000 | $59,000 | $72,000 |
| **4-year private college will cost approximately** | $59,000 | $68,000 | $83,000 | $102,000 | $125,000 | $153,000 |

the country give more than 100,000 academic scholarships yearly.

- In a recent year, over 1 million students received more than $1 billion in need-based state aid.
- Education costs are rising faster than inflation. For the past several years, private college costs have increased two to three times faster than the consumer price index (inflation rate), with public college costs rising only slightly less rapidly. The 1990-91 school year will see tuition increases from 5 to 11 percent. While Princeton's cost is $20,498, up 6.7 percent, Yale is a close second at $19,310, with a predicted annual rise of 7 percent.
- By the year 2000, a college education will cost more than $100,000 for a four-year school.
- Fifty-two percent of financial support for college comes from loans, 44 percent from grants, and about 4 percent from work/study programs. Compare this to a decade ago when 80 percent of student aid came from grants and only 17 percent from loans with the remaining 3 percent from work/study programs.

- If your child will begin college in the year 2000, in order to pay for a four-year education at a public school, you need to start saving about $300 each month beginning now in order to pay his/her costs (based on an 8 percent annual pretax return on your investment). For a private four-year college, you need to start investing almost $650 every month.
- According to U.S. Census Bureau estimates, when compared to high school graduates, male college graduates averaged 46 percent more in salary and female college graduates more than 70 percent more in salary, in their first 10 years of work.
- According to the College Board, 10 years ago 54 percent of colleges offered merit awards without regard to family income. Today that figure is up to 86 percent.
- About 5 million students received student aid for the academic year 1989-90.
- The year 1990 will produce 2530 college graduates representing $70,416,390 in tuition, room and board costs. (Source: *Money* magazine, "America's Best College Buys, Fall '90".)
- For the academic year 1990-91: The federal government will award $13.2 billion in subsidized loans and another $6.5 billion in grants; Colleges will award $5.5 billion in financial aid and tuition discount programs; States will pay out $1.7 billion in student aid.
- Almost 50 percent of all college students receive some form of economic assistance (public or private) today.

## WARNING: DON'T BELIEVE EVERYTHING YOU HEAR OR READ

One of the most misunderstood beliefs about scholarships is that the money awarded from them can be as good as money in your pocket. This is not true. While it is true that a scholarship can help pay your college bill, or replace a loan or a work opportunity in your financial aid package, it will not change either the parent's or student's expected contribution. Those amounts have been set by the need analysis formula and remain constant.

For example, if the total family contribution has been determined to be $5,000 and the college costs $8,000, there is a remaining $3,000 that needs to be met. A $1,000 scholarship will reduce that need to $2,000. That leaves less money that the financial aid officer will have to come up with in grants, work/study, loans or other aid alternatives. The family still needs to contribute $5,000 toward these total costs.

The only exception we have found where a scholarship directly affects the family contribution is where a "no need" scholarship is awarded to a student who has been found to have no need according to his need analysis. In this case the money goes directly to the student or the family. An example of this is where the family contribution at a college that costs $6,000 has been set at $6,000. There is no "remaining need" as far as the financial aid determination is concerened. The family pays the entire bill at this college. Along comes a $2,500 scholarship. This award shrinks the family contribution to $3,500.

There is also the common bellief that there are thousands of one-of-a-kind scholarships that go unclaimed each year. It is true that many scholarships do remain unclaimed. However the main reason is that they are either so obscure or have such specialized requirements, that only a few students could qualify. Our advice is to search for your scholarships through traditional routes, rather than look for off-beat, one-of-a-kind "special" scholarships that have these long lists of unusual, particular criteria making them nearly impossible to meet.

Scholarships are an important source of free money and should not be overlooked and you do have a chance of receiving a special award if you make the effort to find these sources yourself. Here are some steps to help you begin your search:

- Check with financial aid officers and high school counselors.
- Check with your family about past job and service affiliations.
- Check with your community.
- Check with the college admissions offices and college administrators where you are applying.
- Check with the national scholarship organizations.

- Check the books, guides, directories, and newsletters at your public library.
- Check with state scholarship commissions.
- Check with state departments of education.

After you have checked into these sources and the other avenues to free money described in this book, you can dig even further into the vast scholarship bank by looking for those "special" unique awards (see Appendix III for individual sources and reference directories).

How often have you seen those ads by companies claiming to be able to get you all the money you need for college within 90 days or they will refund 100 percent of your money? These computerized scholarship search firms "guarantee" to help students find private agency aid programs for which they might be eligible. We have found the value and costs of these services to vary considerably. Unless the service has a extraordinarily complete, up-to-date data base (which you have no way of checking), including all necesssary information for application, eligibility requirements, and most important, deadlines, it probablly won't be of any more use than your high school guidance counselor or the financial aid officers at the schools you are applying to. The reference sources at your local library can also be a tremendous aid to tracking down these scholarships and grants, as well as information on federal and state programs for which you are eligible.

In addition, remember these college palnning and financial aid services are operating on an extremely high profit margin. Many entrepreneur, business opportunity, and franchise publications even advertise that you can make up to 300 percent profit by running a scholarship/financial aid matching service. We recommend you save the fees (their profits), which can be as high as $500, and do the legwork yourself. You probably will get better results. And it won't cost you anything.

# CHAPTER 1

# FINANCIAL AID AND HOW TO APPLY FOR IT

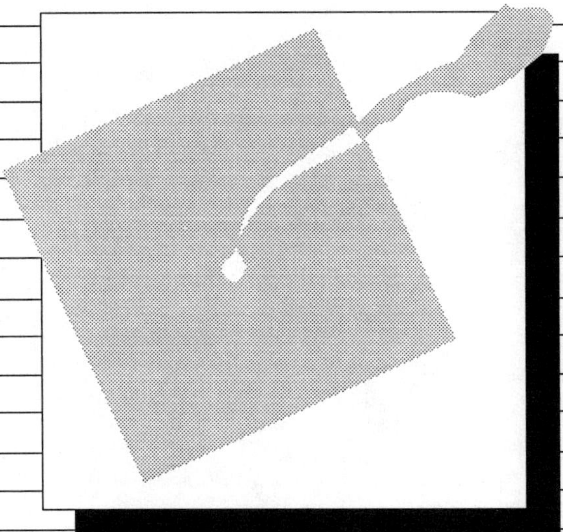

# FINANCIAL AID AND HOW TO APPLY FOR IT

## WHAT IS FINANCIAL AID?

Student Financial Aid is help in meeting the costs of a college education. Student aid comes from the U.S. government (both federal and state), colleges, and private agencies. There are several types of aid available including educational loans, scholarships, work/study programs, and grants.

A student's eligibility to receive aid is determined by a very specific formula, which is called a need analysis. This formula takes into consideration the student's and the parents' taxable income, the family assets and college costs (we will explain what makes up college costs later). What results is the student's need and the family contribution. The concept of need does not mean the same thing as "needy." Financial need is a number determined by a complex set of mathematical formulas and figuring, specified by the United States Congress and written into federal law. You can get a booklet describing the family contribution formula in detail by writing to: Congressional Methodology, Department M-11, Pueblo, CO, 81009-0015. (Although need is determined by formula, under certain circumstances the financial aid administrator can adjust—up or down—your family contribution or your cost of education if he/she believes your familys' financial circumstances warrant it.)

The family contribution is the amount the parents and student are expected to contribute towards the total costs. Any remaining costs are paid through financial aid, i.e., a combination of grants, scholarships, or work/study programs. If these fail to add up to the total costs, then the "remaining need" will have to be made up in the form of low-interest loans. Once the family contribution has been determined, it always remains the same in the need analysis. What varies greatly are the individual costs of the colleges the student has chosen in his selection of where he wants to go. Since the amount and mix of funds available to individual students varies from school to school, more than one college should be considered.

**Chart 2**
**Determining Family Contribution**

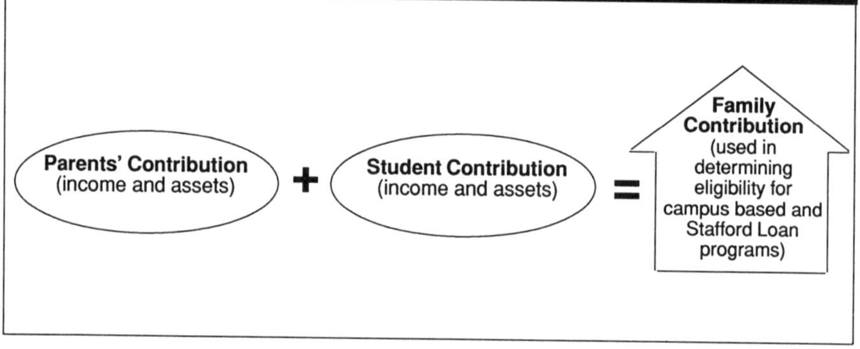


**Chart 3**
**Determining Financial Need**
**(must be calculated separately for each school applied to)**

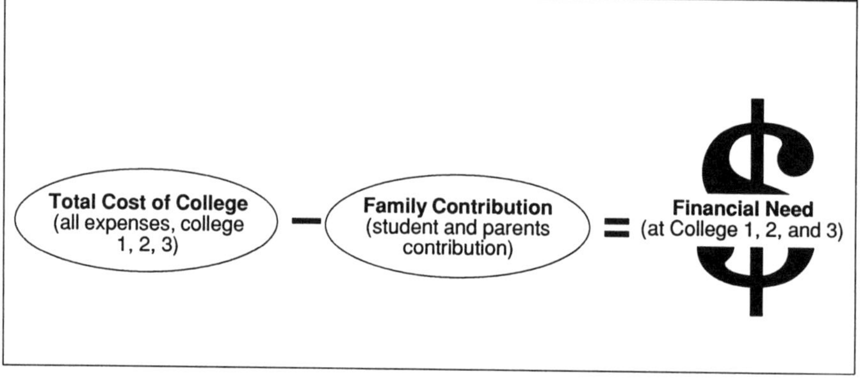

**Chart 4**
**Determining "Remaining Need"**

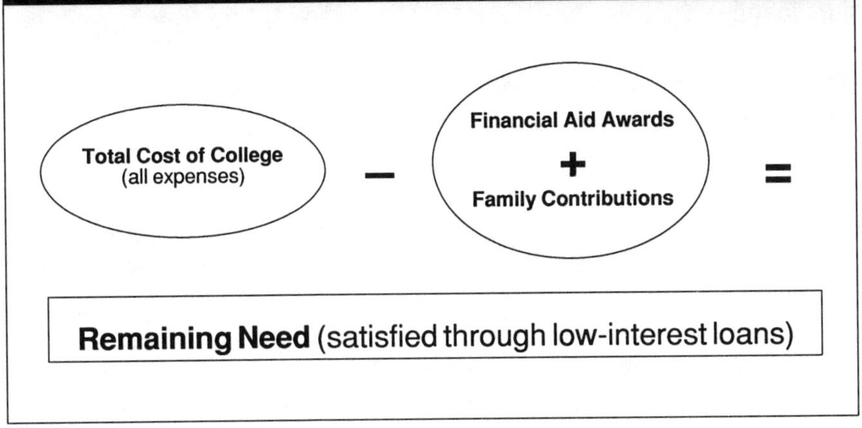


## HOW MUCH DOES A YEAR AT COLLEGE COST?

When determining your college costs be as liberal as possible. This will put you in the position of being able to get the greatest amount of free money possible.

*The greater the overall expense for the student, the greater is the possibility of proving financial aid need.*

In other words, the amount of aid given is in accordance with the student's statement of officially defined financial need.

The financial aid application forms refer to this as "student expense budget." A student should consider all possible expenses when determining this, including:

***Tuition and fees.*** These vary from college to college, the biggest difference being between public and private institutions. Tuition is the charge for instruction. Fees can include services such as health, library, student activities, etc.

***Books and supplies.*** Depending on the courses chosen, the cost of books, paper, etc., will vary. Supplies for laboratory, computer, engineering, and art classes, for example, may raise the cost of supplies significantly.

***Housing.*** This depends on whether a student plans to live at home, in a student dorm, or off-campus in an apartment (or fraternal organization) or other student housing.

***Meals.*** Food costs vary in different areas of the country. A student may choose a school meal plan, eat most of his meals at home, or cook for himself.

***Personal expenses.*** These include clothing, insurance, social outings, long-distance telephone calls, and any out-of-pocket expenses, depending on the student's expected lifestyle while at college.

***Transportation.*** If a student lives on-campus, transportation costs will be minor. If a student lives off-campus, daily commuting expenses (i.e., bus fare, gas, ride sharing) must be considered. Costs for maintaining a personal car for a student living off-campus can make a difference in his/her budget. Also, depending how far from home college is, costs for round-trip travel during vacation times and summer can vary greatly.

***Medical care, disability, extra insurance.*** These are also important considerations in figuring the total budget for the nine-month school year.

***Married with (or without children).*** This can also make an obvious difference in a student's overall budget and is considered when being awarded a student aid package.

Most schools include detailed costs for attendance in their catalogues and brochures. In addition, the College Board's *The College Cost Book* or the ACT's *College Planning/Search Book* are good guides for working out college cost estimates (see Appendix III).

Chart 5

**Approximate Yearly College Expenses** (national estimates)

| Type of School | 1991-92 | | 1992-93 | | 1993-94 | |
|---|---|---|---|---|---|---|
| | Lives On-Campus | Off-Campus | On-Campus | Off-Campus | On-Campus | Off-Campus |
| **2-year school (public)** | $6,500 | $4,600 | $7,000 | $5,000 | $7,600 | $5,400 |
| **2-year school (private)** | $11,800 | $9,800 | $12,700 | $10,600 | $13,800 | $11,400 |
| **4-year school (public)** | $7,600 | $5,700 | $8,200 | $6,100 | $8,800 | $6,600 |
| **4-year school (private)** | $15,700 | $13,700 | $17,000 | $14,800 | $18,400 | $16,000 |

## Chart 6
## Estimated Living Expenses (including tuition and fees)

| California College (9-month school term) | Single Student Living at Home | Single Student Living on Campus | Single Student Living in Own Apartment |
|---|---|---|---|
| California State University, Chico (rural community, State College) | $3,700 | $6,000 | $6,500 |
| California State University, Los Angeles (large metropolitan city, state college | $3,700 | $7,002 | $7,840 |
| University of California at Los Angeles (university system) | $7,392 | $8,782 | $10,612 |
| University of California, Irvine (university system) | $5,820 | $9,420 | $9,420 |
| Pepperdine University (Malibu—private university, 4-year) | $14,666 | $21,506 | $22,236 |
| University of Southern California (private university, 4-year) | $18,964 | $22,842 | $23,706 |

## Chart 7
## Example Worksheet for College Expenses

| | College 1 | College 2 | College 3 |
|---|---|---|---|
| **Tuition and Fees** | | | |
| **Books and Supplies** | | | |
| **Housing (at home, on campus, off campus)** | | | |
| **Transportation (long distance trips home, daily commuting)** | | | |
| **Personal Expenses** | | | |
| **Additional misc. (i.e., medical care, disability, extra insurance, lab fees, fraternity/sorority dues** | | | |
| **Child care (if applicable)** | | | |

## Chart 8
## Examples of Room and Board Charges Four-year Postsecondary Institution (1989-90)

| Name of School | Room | Board | No. of meals per week |
|---|---|---|---|
| Calif. Lutheran University (private) | $2,000 | $2,000 | 21 |
| Calif. State Univ.—Fresno | 1,636 | 1,685 | 14 |
| Calif. State Univ.—Long Beach | 2,990 | 1,238 | 12 |
| Calif. State Univ.–Sacramento | 2,140 | 1,688 | 15 |
| Harvey Mudd College (private) | 2,590 | 2,700 | 19 |
| Pepperdine Univ. (private) | 3,770 | 2,450 | 19 |
| Stanford Univ. (private) | 2,752 | 2,992 | 19 |
| Univ. of Calif.—Los Angeles | 4,375 (combined room & board costs) | | 19 |
| Univ. of Calif.—San Diego | 2,521 | 2,779 | 14 |
| Univ. of Calif.—Santa Barbara | 4,736 | 1,500 | 20 |
| Loyola Marymount Univ. (private) | 2,652 | 2,028 | 20 |

Source 1: Reprinted from "College Costs 1989-90," U.S. Dept. of Education, National Center for Education Statistics.

As can be seen from the above sampling of a few private and public colleges in California, room and board costs vary considerably from school to school, often depending on location (city or rural), real estate values, number of meals offered. When compared to the cost of living at home as a "commuter" student, the savings can make a big difference in the overall student expense budget for the academic year.

# HOW AND WHERE TO LOOK FOR FREE MONEY

Although the free money described in the next chapters does "grow on trees," i.e., is there for the asking, it does have to be "picked," and that takes some effort.

Free money (scholarships and grants), as well as other forms of student aid, is awarded to those students deemed the most deserving, whether through actual need or demonstrated talent (academic, athletic, etc.). Applications need to be sent for and budgets prepared. The application forms must be properly, honestly, and painstakingly filled out. If you make false or dishonest statements regarding income, assets, etc., you run the risk of being discovered in a lie and losing all future chances of receiving aid. Negotiations and acceptances must be followed through in order to make the free money appear. Without following all the steps in their proper order, it can't and won't happen.

Although literally thousands of sources of aid exist in this country, there is lack of coherent, cohesive information on how to find them. Discovering these sources, their requirements, applications, deadlines, etc., can be extremely complicated, time consuming, and confusing. Once the financial aid package is determined, it is entirely possible that the aid officer may have missed or may not be aware of a particular scholarship or loan available to a specially qualified student. If a student thinks he may be eligible for additional aid that may have been overlooked, he is going to have to search out that possibility for himself. This means looking for free money before the financial aid package is actually awarded.

Your search for discovering these special sources should include:

- Talking to your high school guidance counselor.
- Checking school and public libraries for books and pamphlets about aid sources.
- Finding out if your parents belong to any professional or fraternal organizations that might offer aid.
- Finding out about military benefits.

- Investigating community, civic, cultural, and fraternal groups and organizations.
- Looking out for contests and competitions awarding money, and/or scholarships.
- Checking with local businesses, industries, and religious organizations about educational aids.
- Looking for award notices from state and federal agencies about award programs.
- Basically, going after any and all possibilities for private sources of money.

## Chart 9
## Available Sources of Student Aid

PARENTS
PELL GRANT
STAFFORD GRANT
SUPPLEMENTAL EDUCATIONAL OPPORTUNITY GRANT (SEOG)
COLLEGE/WORK STUDY PROGRAM
PERKINS LOAN
STATE SCHOLARSHIP OR GRANT
COLLEGE SCHOLARSHIP OR GRANT
COLLEGE LOAN
PRIVATE SCHOLARSHIP OR GRANT
PRIVATE LOAN (ex. SLS, PLUS)
FULL- OR PART-TIME EMPLOYMENT
SAVINGS
SPOUSAL SUPPORT
GI/VETERANS BENEFITS
SOCIAL SECURITY

# HOW TO APPLY FOR FINANCIAL AID

There are two main companies that provide need analysis: THE AMERICAN COLLEGE TESTING PROGRAM (ACT)* and the COLLEGE SCHOLARSHIP SERVICE (CSS). Most colleges accept the analysis by one of these services. The CSS processes the Financial Aid Form (FAF), and the ACT processes the Family Financial Statement (FFS). These forms can be obtained from the colleges where you plan to apply or from your high school guidance office.

If you are applying for federal aid, use the free Application for Federal Student Aid (AFSA). Some colleges do not use the FFS or the FAF. They may either use only the federal form (AFSA) or a state application form similar to the FAF or FFS. For example, the PHEAA form used in Pennsylvania or the Student Aid Application for California (SAAC). (See Appendix IV for examples of some of these forms).

Once the completed applications are received, they are processed by the appropriate need analysis service, sent back to the college, and evaluated by the college FINANCIAL AID OFFICER. The financial aid officer determines whether a student is eligible for financial aid by reviewing the need analysis report in depth and from that point builds a FINANCIAL AID PACKAGE for the student.

After deducting the family contribution (an important factor is whether a student is classified as dependent or independent), the financial aid officer awards varying combinations of GRANTS, LOANS, SCHOLARSHIPS, and work/study programs (where the college gives students part-time jobs to help pay the expenses for school). This constitutes the financial aid package, which when added to the FAMILY CONTRIBUTION should cover 100 percent of the costs of attending one year of college.

Students are notified of the results of the financial aid package in the form of an award letter, which includes details of the proposed award. This letter must be carefully examined and responded to in order to safeguard the aid in a student's name.

In most cases, grants and scholarships are the best types of financial aid awards, simply because they do not have to be paid back. They are gifts.

If a student or his family finds that it is difficult to meet their assigned contribution, it is often possible to work out a special payment plan

*Terms in uppercase type can be found in the Glossary in Appendix I

through the college or arrange a commercial low-cost loan. The financial aid officer should be able to work with the family in negotiating a package that everyone can live with.

*IMPORTANT NOTE:* Every student should apply for a Pell Grant (see Chapter 4) even if he thinks he will not qualify. In order to be considered for other financial aid programs, most schools require that a student apply for the Pell Grant. This can be done by just checking a box in either the FAF or FFS.

CHART 10

**Important Addresses For Financial Aid Applications, Processing and Information**

College Scholarship Service (FAF)
Box 2700
Princeton, NJ 08541
or
Box 70
Berkeley, CA 94701

American College Testing Program (FFS)
P.O. Box 168
Iowa City, IA 52240

Federal Student Aid Programs (AFSA)
Box 92831
Los Angeles, CA 90009
or
Public Documents Distribution Center
DEA-84
Pueblo, CO 81009

Higher Education Assistance Foundation
P.O. Box 6407
St. Paul, MN 55164

continued. . .

Guaranteed Student Loan Program
U.S. Department of Education
Washington, D.C. 20202

Sources of Information on Student Aid
National Education Association
1201 16th Street, N.W.
Washington, D.C. 20036

## CHART 11
## Financial Aid Application Forms and Services

Free forms (available at public libraries, the financial aid office of schools, high school guidance offices):

- The U.S. Department of Education's "Application for Federal Student Aid" (AFSA).
- The Pennsylvania Higher Education Assistance Agency's (PHEAA's) "Application for Pennsylvania State Grant and Federal Student Aid."
- The Illinois State Scholarship Commission's "Application for Federal and State Student Aid" (AFSSA).
- The United Student Aid Funds' (USAF's) "Singlefile Form."*

Forms used in applying for non-federal aid (charge processing fee):

- The College Scholarship Service's "Financial Aid Form" (FAF).
- The American College Testing Program's "Family Financial Statement" (FFS).

continued. . .

- The Student Aid Application for California (SACC).
- The Higher Education Assistance Foundation (HEAF).*

WARNING:
All forms listed can be used for applying for federal aid, but individual schools may require a specific form for applying for nonfederal aid. Check with the schools where you are applying.

* Private nonprofit corporation that guarantees student loans.

## Chart12

**QUESTIONS ABOUT STUDENT AID?**

**call the**

**FEDERAL STUDENT AID INFORMATION CENTER**

**TOLL-FREE**

**1-(800)-333-INFO**

**9:00 a.m.—5:30 p.m.**
**Eastern Time**
**Mon.—Fri.**

# WHAT IF YOU ARE AN "INDEPENDENT" STUDENT?

There are several important criteria that a student applying for financial aid must meet in order to qualify for "independent" status. If you meet these criteria, your parents' income and financial assets will not be considered when determining financial aid eligibility.

You are automatically considered an independent student if you:

- Are at least 24 years old by December 31 of the award year.
- Are a veteran of the U.S. Armed Forces.
- Are an orphan or ward of the court.
- Have legal dependants other than a spouse and pay at least half of his/her support.

If you are a single undergraduate student (not meeting any of the above criteria) and have earned at least $4,000 (both taxed and untaxed) for the past two calendar years and have not been claimed as a dependent on your parents' tax returns for the previous two calendar years, you may qualify. Also, if you are married and are no longer being claimed as a dependent by your parents, you may qualify for independent status.

If you claim to be an independent student, you may be asked to prove it before you are awarded any federal student aid. The aid administrator at your school has the authority to change your status (if you think you have a special circumstance) from dependent to independent. This decision is based on their opinion and the decision is final. There are no appeals. The contribution of an independent student is based on two factors only: the student's income and assets.

# UNDERSTANDING YOUR FINANCIAL AID PACKAGE

The financial aid package will come in the form of an award letter from the colleges you have applied to. At this time you need to carefully evaluate and determine with your family which package is best for you. It is also the time you should contact the financial aid officer(s) to discuss any specific questions and renegotiate any awards, payment plans, etc., and make any revisions you feel you deserve.

The letter will state how much aid you can expect in grants or loans and how much in a work/study program. The first part of a student aid package consists of what you are eligible to receive under the federal PELL GRANT and your state aid program. Next are the federally funded programs administered through the colleges, the COLLEGE WORK/STUDY Program, the Perkins Loan Program and the Supplemental Educational Opportunity Grant Program (SEOG). (These are explained in later chapters.)

Be aware that your award may come with restrictions such as the necessity to maintain a certain grade point average. Also, some scholarships and loans and all grants are awarded on a yearly basis and may or may not be renewable.

Following the federal programs are those financed by the schools themselves, the loan and scholarship programs. Keep in mind that some schools have considerably more money available for student aid than others. Their endowments give them greater flexibility and independence in making awards.

Finally, the financial aid package will incorporate any outside scholarships you have received (or anticipate receiving) as reported by you to your financial aid officer. You risk losing all your awards if you or your family do not accurately and completely report your current and potential financial situation.

There are several ways in which your school can treat outside scholarships. They may reduce the gift aid (grants or scholarships from the school), the work/study portion of aid, or partially reduce both. Or they may apply the scholarship to the aid package if there is "remaining need" that has not previously been fully met. If all portions of the aid package are met by the scholarship, any remaining money may be used to reduce part of the family contribution.

In any case your assigned family contribution always remains the same. As we will explain in Chapter 3, if you are awarded a "no-need" award and it has been determined that you have no need, i.e., your family contribution is 100 percent of the cost of education, the money from a scholarship is yours to use to reduce the cost of school. A no need award given to a student who has established need will be used to reduce the student's need portion of the package as decided by your financial aid officer.

*Any aid, whether awarded privately, through a state or federal program or college, cannot total more than the cost of education.*

The normal "grace" period in which you have to accept an award package is 10 to 14 days. You must sign and return a copy of the letter as your acceptance of the award. You can accept all or part of the aid, or you can request the revisions you feel you would like. If you do not reply by the requested date, you may lose your awards altogether. Financial aid dollars are in great demand and short supply. Your money will go to someone else if you do not respond in accordance with their instructions.

## YOUR CHECKLIST FOR FINANCIAL AID

### *I. How to Determine Your Costs:*

- ❑ Decide on which schools will best meet your future educational and career goals. Consider all options including the military academies and service opportunities.
- ❑ Write to those schools for catalogs, admissions applications, financial aid opportunities, etc.
- ❑ Using these materials (and any other cost information obtained from Admissions Offices), develop budgets for each school. Include all living expenses.
- ❑ Check with athletic coaches and other department officials about available sources of college funds.

## *II. Filling Out Forms and Deadlines*

- ❑ Check admission deadlines.
- ❑ Check financial aid deadlines for all sources to which you will be applying.
- ❑ Decide which *need analysis* form to file: the Financial Aid Form (FAF) processed by the College Scholarship Service and the Family Financial Statement (FFS) processed by the American College Testing program are accepted by most colleges.
- ❑ Carefully fill out and complete all portions of the need analysis form.
- ❑ Make copies of everything you submit in regard to admissions and financial aid.
- ❑ Send all important forms and documents by certified mail.
- ❑ Apply for federal student financial aid (Pell Grant by checking the appropriate box on the FAF or FFS form or you can use the Federal AFSA form).
- ❑ Check with guidance counselor or financial aid officer regarding a state scholarship or grant application and which additional forms, if any, are necessary to submit for state aid.
- ❑ Keep all correspondence received from need analysis services and financial aid offices. Read acknowledgements thoroughly to make sure all forms have been accepted and are being processed.
- ❑ If additional information is requested, provide this information as soon as possible so that processing of your application will not be interrupted or canceled.
- ❑ Forward copies of Student Aid Report to colleges to which you are applying.

## *III. Financial Aid Package and Award Letter*

- ❑ The award letter(s) will state amount of grant aid offered by the school, loan aid offered and work/study aid. Carefully read your award letter(s) and review all parts of your financial aid package including:

  A. If there is a loan portion included in your package, review terms of payment, conditions of funding, requirements, etc. Apply for loans after you have accepted admission to school.

  B. Amount of work-study aid.

  C. Grant aid offered.

- ❑ Choose which school you want to attend on the combined basis of economic feasibility and career/educational goals.

- ❑ Notify the school of your formal acceptance of their offer for admission and let other schools know about your decision not to attend so that financial aid funds reserved for you can be released.

## *IV. Researching and Applying for Private Scholarships*

- ❑ Check your high school library and local library for additional sources of financial aid. There are many detailed books, reports, and pamphlets describing private scholarship and grant programs.

- ❑ Ask your high school guidance counselor about any sources of private scholarship or loan aid he/she knows of.

- ❑ Research all personal avenues and possibilities of aid through your parents' affiliations, memberships, community organizations, veterans benefits, Social Security benefits, minority opportunities, academic, leadership, and special talent opportunities.

## *V. Alternative Payment Plans*

Investigate any and all of the following alternative financing plans available at the college you have chosen:

- ❑ Pre-payment plans.
- ❑ Discount tuition plans.
- ❑ Multiple family member plans.
- ❑ Alumni plans.
- ❑ Fee waivers for special student categories.
- ❑ Credit card plans.
- ❑ Deferred or installment plans.

# CHAPTER 2

## SCHOLARSHIPS: FREE MONEY BECAUSE YOU'RE GOOD AT SOMETHING

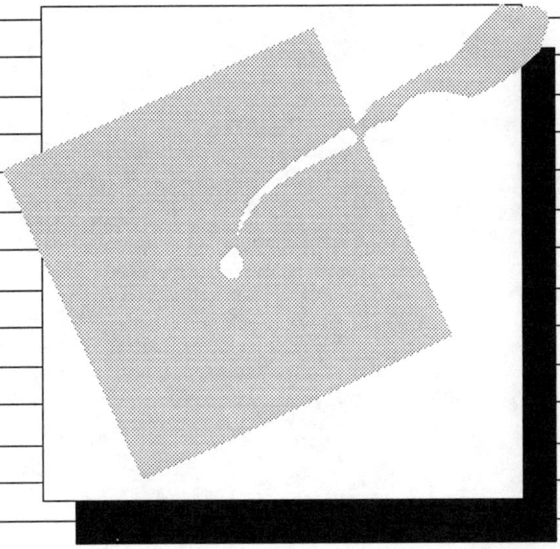

# SCHOLARSHIPS: FREE MONEY BECAUSE YOU'RE GOOD AT SOMETHING

Scholarships can be an excellent source of funds, and it is worth the time and effort it takes to become the recipient of a scholarship award. In addition they often add prestige and luster to a graduate's resumé. However, scholarships can be difficult to obtain because they are awards that do not have to be paid back.

Scholarships can be awarded by colleges, states, the federal government (military scholarships), and private agencies. There are several types of scholarships.

1. Those awarded by a particular college.
2. National scholarships for use at any college.
3. Scholarships based on need.
4. Scholarships awarded without consideration for need (i.e., academics, special abilities, or talents).
5. Scholarships that are awarded for one time only (nonrenewable), and those that are renewable yearly.

It is important to remember that scholarship awards do not reduce the family contribution, which has been set by the need analysis process. In the financial aid package, the family contribution always stays the same. A scholarship will help pay the college bill, but not reduce the parents' or child's designated contribution.

Scholarships based on "need" are awarded only to students who have demonstrated "need" through the analysis of the financial aid officer at the college. If the family contribution is equal to the costs of attending college, then the scholarship will not be given, since no need exists. However, if the costs of college exceed the family contribution and need is established (whatever amount), the need-based scholarship will be awarded to help pay the costs not covered by the family.

Scholarships awarded on a "no-need" basis are different. They can be given regardless of a student's financial need. Winning a $1,000 no-need academic scholarship will reduce the costs of college by just that amount. If the family has demonstrated need, the money will be used to cover part or sometimes even all of the need portion of the financial aid package. If the no-need scholarship is awarded to a student whose family has no need, the money goes directly to the family or student. For example, if the family contribution has been set at $6,000 and the school costs $6,000 then the "no-need" award will shrink the family contribution by whatever is the amount of the scholarship. If the cost of college is $8,000 and the family contribution is $4,000, the student's need is $4,000. If the scholarship award is $3,000, then the need is reduced from $4,000 to $1,000. If the award is as high as $4,000, the family contribution remains the same, but the entire need is wiped out by the scholarship.

## ACADEMIC MERIT SCHOLARSHIPS

Scholarships based on academic achievement are highly competitive. The largest source of academic scholarships are colleges and universities. Over 1,200 institutions offer this type of scholarship, generally of the no-need type, to students who meet high criteria in their grade point average, test scores, or class ranking. In the 1980s the amount of merit money awarded by selective liberal arts colleges grew by more than 300 percent. As we mentioned, check with your high school counselor, student aid officer, and instructors in your major field of study for scholarship sources. They will be able to advise you of scholarships from both private and public institutions. Keep an eye on the bulletin boards in their offices for notices of scholarships and their deadlines.

For example, in a recent year, Duke University awarded 26 freshmen no-need scholarships averaging more than $10,000. Boston University offered $3,000 a year for four years to several hundred undecided students with high averages (B or better) who had been accepted for attendance but had not been given aid. Syracuse University, after sending out its acceptances, offered $2,000 a year for four years to 700 students in the top 10 percent of their applicants and who did not qualify for aid.

Academic scholarships are also awarded by community organizations, businesses, labor unions, churches, professional groups, or national foundations. These funds are often harder to locate than those from the large federal programs. Patriotic, civic, and fraternal organizations, religious and ethnic groups, and social and professional clubs will be able to advise you of funds through their local chapters or national headquarters.

Estimates of unclaimed scholarships run as high as $140 million for one year. These dollars are there for the asking. However, you must find them, and that's why investigating all possible sources of this free money is not only important, it's absolutely necessary. We've listed several individual sources and their addresses as well as reference guides and directories (See Appendix III). You can find many of these sources at your local bookstores, public and school libraries. Make sure their copies are current as most are updated yearly.

Remember, once you've located a scholarship, you will need to prove you're deserving of the funds. In addition to academic achievement, some may require essay writing, autobiographies, or getting recommendations. Your leadership ability, heritage, and other factors may be considered along with your grade point average.

## THE NATIONAL MERIT SCHOLARSHIP PROGRAM: COAST TO COAST MONEY

This is one of the most well known private scholarship programs in the country. It is a nationwide program in which over 1 million students compete each year for more than $21 million in scholarships. There are several subprograms within the national program with varying types of awards and amounts. All students participating in these programs take the PSAT/NMSQT (Preliminary Scholastic Aptitude Test/National Merit Scholarship Qualifying Test), usually in their junior year of high school. Approximately 50,000 applicants receive citations for high performance. A total of 5,800 awards are given to the top finalists in the competition.

## *National Merit Scholarships*

Eighteen hundred students a year receive nonrenewable, no-need awards of $1,000, while 4,200 students receive renewable scholarships ranging from $250 to $8,000.

## *National Achievement Scholarship Program for Outstanding Negro Students (Evanston, IL)*

This program is for outstanding black secondary students. The 1,200 finalists in this program compete for 700 scholarships (350 nonrenewable awards at $2,000 and 350 renewable awards between $250 and $8,000).

## *National Hispanic Scholar Awards Program*

As of 1984, Hispanics participating in the program are eligible to receive scholarships ($1,500 awards). This program is sponsored by the College Board and funded by the Mellon Foundation. In addition to academic achievement, community involvement and personal leadership qualities are considered.

## *Corporate Merit Scholarships*

More than 1,500 renewable, need-based awards (between $250-$4,000) are given by over 400 corporations for employees' children, residents of corporate locales, or future majors in areas of corporate interest who are Merit Program finalists.

Examples of some national corporations that participate in the Corporate Merit Scholarship program or a general Merit Scholarship program for employees' children are: IBM, Westinghouse, General Mills, Food Fair, Coca Cola, State Farm, Firestone Tire, and the Ford Motor Company.

### *College Merit Scholarships*

More than 200 colleges sponsor need-based Merit Scholarships (at $2,000 each) for students applying to participating schools.

## OTHER SCHOLARSHIP PROGRAMS

### *FEEA Fund Scholarships*

Two hundred Federal Employee Education and Assistance (FEEA) Fund Scholarships (between $500-$2,500) are awarded to federal employees and members of their families each year.

### *National Honor Society*

This national program is run by school teachers and administrators belonging to the local high school chapter of the Society. They nominate students for the honor roll. The Society selects from among these nominees and makes 250 one-time awards of $1,000.

### *Presidential Scholars*

One hundred twenty students are selected from students who are high scorers on the ACT and SAT. A four-day visit to Washington, D.C., and a $1,000 check from a private foundation is presented to each student.

### *Robert C. Byrd Honors Scholarship Program*

This is a federally funded program administered by the states. Each state establishes its own criteria and selection; however, the majority are awarded to students who have demonstrated outstanding academic achievement in high school and show promise of continued academic achievement in college. The awards are not based on need and can be used at any school. These $1,500 nonrenewable scholarships are awarded for the first year of study following high school graduation.

## *Harry S. Truman Scholarship*

This is also a federally funded program for students already in college. More than 100 awards are made each year up to $7,000 per year for junior, senior, and graduate work. Consideration is given for those students interested in public service careers.

## *Westinghouse Science Talent Search*

This is a national program with awards given to high school students for outstanding research projects in science, mathematics, or engineering judged at science fairs around the country. The awards are based on 1,000-word reports submitted by the students on the projects, teacher recommendations, and standardized test scores. The top 100 awards range from $10,000 to $40,000. Runners-up receive $1,000.

## *National 4H Awards Program, Future Homemakers of America and Boy Scouts of America*

More examples of national scholarship programs in which students can participate are through local 4H Clubs (more than $250,000 total awards ranging from $1,000 to $1,500), FHA chapters or the Boy Scout organization.

## *National Basketball Association Scholarships*

The NBA offers $50,000 in scholarships to high school seniors based on extra curricular activities, test scores, teacher recommendations, and essay competition, without regard to athletic ability.

## *Essay Writing and Scholarship Contests*

There are many national contests for scholarships, usually offering small money prizes. The National Association of Secondary School Principals (Reston, VA) publishes a booklet of over 60 competitions that they endorse as reputable and sound. For example, the Mensa organization awards prizes to $1,000 based on essay competition. The Voice of America Scholarship program (VFW National Headquarters, Kansas City, MO) makes national and local awards from $1,000 to $14,000 based on delivery of three to five minute original scripts. Broadcast Music, Inc. (BMI) awards between $500 and $2,500 to student composers who enter their awards competition by submitting original musical compositions.

## SCHOLARSHIPS FROM YOUR STATE

Most states now grant scholarships for academic achievement to students attending a college or university within the state. Some states grant scholarships with merit as the primary criterion. These awards are not affected by need. Others grant scholarships based on need, with a high grade point average necessary for eligibility. A third type of scholarship is based on academic accomplishment, but if a student does not demonstrate financial need, the scholarship is given honorarily with no money actually being funded. A few states provide assistance to residents attending college out-of-state. Funding for merit-based programs is increasing more rapidly than need-based programs, as states face stiffer competition to keep their best students from attending college out-of-state.

Generally a state will have several small scholarship programs, such as programs for veterans, veterans' children, educational studies, children and spouses of state employees', nursing or health care studies. These are competitive programs with students displaying the highest qualifications receiving the awards. One example is the Law Enforcement Personnel Dependents Scholarships given to needy dependents and spouses of California police and other law enforcement officers, firefighters, and other related county, city, and state employees who have been injured or killed in the performance of duty. To find out about state sponsored scholarships contact your state department of education or financial aid officer.

# PRIVATE SCHOLARSHIP SOURCES: CHECK OUT WHO YOU ARE, WHERE YOU CAME FROM, AND WHAT'S AROUND YOU

In addition to the previous scholarships, there are many other sources of privately funded money. The following are examples of some of the programs offering awards based on ability, affiliation, fields of study, interests, career choice, athletics, community service, etc. (Refer to Appendix III for addresses.)

## *Membership in Unions*

Union scholarships include awards to children of members belonging to:

- The ILGWU (International Ladies Garment Workers Union) (up to $2,500 for four years).
- The International Association of Machinists.
- The United Steelworkers of America.
- The International Brotherhood of Teamsters.
- The Postal Workers Union.

## *Leadership/Community Service*

These include awards given by:

- The Josten Foundation (administered by the Citizens Scholarship Foundation, awards of approximately $1,000).
- Century III Leaders Scholarship Program (administered by the National Association of Secondary School Principals, Reston, VA); 102 awards of $500 and 102 $1,500 awards, plus two $10,000 national awards.
- The William Randolph Hearst Foundation (San Francisco) funds the U.S. Senate Youth Program. More than 100 awards at $2,000, plus a week's stay in Washington, D.C., offered to high school juniors and seniors who are student government officers.

- Educational Communications Scholarship Foundation (Lake Forest, IL).
- Soroptimist International of the Americas Youth Citizenship Awards. Forty-three cash awards of merit at $1,250 each, and a $2,000 award to one finalist. Recognizes school and community efforts and achievement and encourages continuing high concepts of patriotism and effective cooperation in home, community, national, and international affairs. Awarded to senior high school students who have, during their high school years, demonstrated service in home, school, and community, dependability, leadership, and a clear sense of purpose. For information check with local Soroptimist club (listed in phone directory, *Chamber of Commerce Directory*, Status of Women Office, city hall, League of Women Voters, or with other agencies.
- Columbian Squires. Two scholarships for entering college freshman at $1,000 each. One must be used at the Catholic University of America; the other at any Catholic university or college. Awards are made on basis of academic excellence. Recipients must be in good standing in the Columbian Squires. For information write to: Knights of Columbus, P.O. Drawer 1670, New Haven, CT 06507.

## *Community Organizations*

These awards are given to students living within the local area of PTA chapters, chambers of commerce, local utility companies, corporations that operate local plants or factories, high schools, service and civic organizations. Check with the individual organizations in your area or the local chapter of Dollars for Scholars for sources of locally raised educational scholarship funds.

## *Fraternal Organizations, Lodges, Civic and Patriotic Associations*

Among the many organizations making awards to members and member's children through their local chapters are:

- Elks National Foundation ($800-$5,000 awards).

- Kiwanis.
- Lions.
- Rotary (Foundation for International Understanding awards).
- Loyal Order of Moose.
- Knights of Columbus.
- Rebekah.
- Beta Sigma Phi.
- United Daughters of the Confederacy.
- International Order of Job's Daughters.
- Soroptimists.

### *Ancestry and Nationality*

These groups prove your family's heritage can make a difference:

- Descendants of Signers of the Declaration of Independence.
- UNICO (Italian) Nationals.
- Japanese American Citizens League.
- The Kusciuszko Foundation (Polish descendents, 50 awards of approximately $1,000).
- Danish Brotherhood of America ($1,000 awards).
- Lithuanian Alliance.
- Sons of Norway.
- Russian Brotherhood Organization.
- Armenian Students Association.

Addresses for these organizations can be found in the *Encyclopedia of Associations* in the reference section of your public library.

## *Minorities*

If you belong to a minority, be sure to investigate the numerous scholarship opportunities available to you including:

- Indian Fellowship Program, Washington, D.C., (Native Americans).
- Indian Health Service Scholarships, Rockville, MD (Native Americans).
- Higher Education Assistance Program (Native Americans).
- National Action Council of Minorities in Engineering (NACME), New York, NY (all minorities).
- Student Opportunity Scholarships for Communican Members of the Presbyterian Church, Louisville, KY ($100-$1,400 awards, all minorities).
- American Dental Hygienists Association, Chicago, IL (awards up to $1,500, all minorities).
- National Science Foundation (graduate studies for all minorities).
- Jackie Robinson Foundation, New York, NY (awards up to $4,000, African-Americans).
- National Hispanic Scholarship Fund ($1,500 awards, Hispanics).
- Educational Services League of United Latin American Citizens (1,000 awards of $500, Hispanics).
- Minority Access to Research Careers (MARC) program through the National Institute of General Medical Sciences, Bethesda, MD (ethnic minorities).
- Legal Training for the Disadvantaged, CLEO Washington, D.C. (all minorities).
- NAACP Roy Wilkins Scholarships (all minorities).
- American Institute of Certified Public Accountants Minority Recruitment, New York, NY (maximum to $1,500, all minorities).
- American Institute of Architects (AIA), Washington, D.C. ($500-$3,500, all minorities).

- Dow Jones Minority Editing Intern Program for College Seniors ($1,000 awards, all minorities).

## *Veterans*

If you have a parent who served in one of the branches of our armed forces check these out:

- AMVETS National Scholarship Program, Latham, MA, awards $1,000/year up to four years for children of veterans who are entering college.
- American Legion, Scholarships for Children of American Military Personnel (SCAMPS) awards scholarships between $2,500-$3,000.
- The Coors Fund and the Reserve Officer Association fund scholarship programs for children of American veterans ($500 awards).

## *Student Employment*

Some companies employing students offer educational scholarships. For example, Burger King offers scholarships after just three weeks of employment (maximum of $2,000 in $200 increments). The Western Golf Association has over $2 million in awards for ex-caddies. Several metropolitan newspapers and newspaper chains, including The Washington Post and Gannett (approximately 100 scholarships at $6,000) offer scholarships to newspaper carriers.

## *Religious Denomination*

Many religious organizations give generous scholarships for higher education including:

- National Presbyterian College Scholarships (175 awards between $500-$2,000).
- Knights of Columbus ($1,000 awards, Catholic).

- The Albert Baker Fund (a loan program funding $1,200-$2,000 for Christian Scientist).
- JWB (Jewish).
- Lutheran Brotherhood (200 awards at $2,000).
- Aid Association for Lutherans (AAL) Scholarships (500 awards at $500, 250 at $2,000).

## MONEY IF YOU CAN THROW IT, BOUNCE IT, HIT IT, LIFT IT, RIDE IT, OR RUN WITH IT: ATHLETIC SCHOLARSHIPS

Outstanding athletes in major sports are sought after by colleges, which entice them with generous scholarships. However, even just better than average athletes in both major and minor sports can tap into a considerable source of financial aid from colleges that are seeking students with the type of ability along with required academic achievement. In addition to football, basketball, baseball, tennis, hockey, and track, if you are a decent jock in sports such as:

> gymnastics, sailing, archery, fencing, rowing, swimming, skiing, volleyball, hockey, golf, LaCrosse, bowling, riflery, soccer, cross-country skiing, badminton, rodeo riding, table tennis, sailing, or crew.
>
> You may have a good chance of receiving an athletic scholarship.

We recommend finding out about individual programs by contacting the college coach at the schools you are applying, who usually is involved in running the program. A school's coach can play a strong and important role in influencing an award of financial aid through an athletic scholarship. Work with your high school guidance counselor and coach in choosing colleges that are best suited to your academic and athletic abilities. Recommendation letters from those who have seen you in action should be sent to the coaches at the schools to which you are applying. Work on building a relationship (through letters, phone calls, interviews) with whoever is most likely to decide on who receives a school's athletic scholarships.

Several good sources of information about athletic award opportunities are:

*The National Directory of College Athletics* has separate editions for men and women. Write to Ray Franks, Box 7068, Amarillo, TX 79114.

*Lovejoy's College Guide.* Monarch Books.

*The Winning Edge: A Complete Guide to Intercollegiate Athletic Programs,* Octameron Associates.

*Chronicle Sports Guide: Intercollegiate Athletics and Scholarships,* Chronicle Guidance Publications, P.O. Box 1190, Moravia, NY 13118.

The Athletic Guidance Center (800) 562-5800 is a specialty athletic scholarship counseling service that charges a $250 fee for their services. They offer a money-back guarantee and do the research, letter writing, and distribute your resume to a network of athletic coaches. As with other scholarship services, check with free sources of information before spending your money.

## MONEY FOR SPECIAL TALENTS (YOUR MOTHER WAS RIGHT, AFTER ALL)

These are awards given to students who have demonstrated ability or talent in a specific academic area. Again, those who have observed these talents and skills first hand can be helpful in locating these awards. These can include coaches, dance teachers, art teachers, bandmasters, private tutors, sponsors, and professional musical or performing companies with whom you've worked. A professional who has nurtured your special talents can play an important role in the award process. They may know about competitions and contests that a college counselor is unaware of.

Examples of awards given for talent and skill include:

*Writing:* Scholastic Writing Awards (Scholastic, Inc., New York, NY).

*Art:* Scholastic Art Awards (Scholastic, Inc., New York, NY).

*Drama:* Thespian Society (high school chapters).

*Photography:* Scholastic Photography Awards (Scholastic, Inc., New York, NY).

*Science:* Westinghouse Science Talent Scholarships (Washington, D.C.).

The Arts Recognition and Talent Search (ARTS), an activity of the National Science Foundation for Advancement in the Arts (Miami, FL), searches out students who have shown excellence in dance, music, theater, visual arts, and writing. All who enter are eligible for scholarships cash awards up to $3,000. Information on applications is available through high school art teachers, counselors, principals, or local community art organizations.

## MONEY FOR CAREER INTERESTS

Many scholarships are available to students who have shown a strong interest in pursuing further studies leading to a specific career. Included in these fields of study are:

*Accounting:* National Society of Public Accountants, $1,000-$2,000.

*Architecture:* American Institute of Architects (AIA), $2,000.

*Art:* Arts Recognition and Talent Search (ARTS) of the National Science Foundation for Advancements of the Arts (NFAA), $500-$3,000.

*Education:* Phi Delta Kappa, Inc. Scholarships,Bloomington, IN, $100-$1,500; Kappa Kappa Gamma Scholarships (for women); Omega Psi Phi Fraternity, Washington, D.C., $300-$1,000.

*Engineering:* National Society of Professional Engineers Scholarships, $1,000; AGC Education and Research Foundation, awards to a maximum of $7,500; Society of Mining Engineers, up to $2,000.

*Fashion:* Emilio Pucci Scholarship at the American College for Applied Arts, Atlanta, GA, $1,000.

*Food Service/Hospitality Management:* The Educational Foundation of the National Restaurant Association, Chicago, IL, $500-$10,000; International Food Service Executives Association, $100-$500.

*Foreign Study:* The Rotary Foundation of the Rotary Club Scholarships for International Understanding.

*Golf Course Maintenance:* Golf Course Superintendent Association of America Scholarship Program.

*Geology:* Geological Society of America, maximum to $1,000.

*Geophysics:* SEG Foundation's Scholarship Committee, $1,000.

*Graphic Arts:* Education Council of the Graphic Arts Industry, Inc.

*History:* NSDAR American History Scholarship, four-year scholarship up to $8,000.

*Home Economics:* AHEA Foundation, $1,000-$5,000.

*Horticulture:* Professional Plant Growers Scholarship Foundation, $1,000-$2,000; American Orchid Society, $100-$10,000; American Horticulture Society.

*Insurance, Business Administration, and Actuarial Mathematics:* Corporate Sponsors Program at the College of Insurance (New York, NY).

*Journalism:* Academy of Television Arts and Sciences, Burbank, CA; Dow Jones Newspaper Fund, Princeton, NJ; Scripps Howard Foundation Scholarships, Cincinnati,OH, up to $3,000.

*Library Science:* Booklet available from the Standing Committee on Library Education.

*Music:* National Federation of Music Clubs.

*Naval Architecture:* Webb Institute of Naval Architecture (all tuition paid to top students scoring high SATs).

*Private Club Management:* Club Managers Association of America, $1,000.

*Public Service:* Public Employees Roundtable, $500-$1,000.

*Real Estate Appraisers:* American Institute of Real Estate Appraisers, $2,000.

*Special Education:* Division of Personnel Preparation, Special Education Programs, Dept. of Education.

*Travel:* American Society of Travel Agents Scholarship Foundation, $750-$1,200.

To find out more details about these and other awards, contact organizations in your particular fields of interest and send for career information. Refer to "Need a Lift?" published by the American Legion, P.O. Box 1050, Indianapolis, IN 46206, or the latest edition of the *Occupational Handbook* issued by the Bureau of Labor Statistics, U.S. Dept. of Labor, or contact the professional membership organizations that serve these careers (they are listed in Vol. I, Gale's Encyclopedia of Associations).

## SCHOLARSHIPS FOR WOMEN ONLY

Scholarships are available exclusively to women in a specific field of study, pursuing a specialized career or for general academic studies. These include:

The National Association of Bank Women (Chicago) awards scholarships to members pursuing a career in banking or business. (Associated with Mundelein College, Chicago.)

AT&T Bell Laboratories (Homedel, NJ); the Society of Women Engineers (New York, NY), University of Missouri-Rolla (Rolla, MO) all offer awards to women pursuing careers in engineering. The Bell Labs scholarships will pay all college costs.

The Women's Western Golf Foundation (Cedarburg, WI), (four-year maximum to $6,000) and the Gloria Fecht Memorial Scholarship Fund (San Dimas, CA), award substantial yearly scholarships ($1,500-$2,500) for women demonstrating a strong interest or ability in golf.

Women's Sports Foundation helps channel the many scholarships available to women athletes. Send for: "Athletic Scholarship Guide" ($2), 342 Madison Ave., Suite 728, New York, NY 10173, which lists over 10,000 athletic scholarships.

America's Junior Miss Pageant (Mobile, AL) awards more than $3 million for winners of their beauty and talent competition.

Kappa Kappa Gamma Fraternity (Columbus, OH) has a scholarship fund for women students working toward a degree in rehabilitation education.

The Whirly-Girls (Alexandria, VA) awards scholarships ($4,000) to aspiring women helicopter pilots.

Business and Professional Women's Foundation (Washington, D.C.) awards scholarships ($1,500)to upgrade skills for career advancement for women 25 years or older.

The Clairol Scholarship Program awarded through the Business and Professional Women's Foundation (Washington, D.C.) is the only nationwide company-sponsored fund for women 30 years of age and older for continuing postsecondary education for the purpose of career advancement (awards up to $1,000).

Additional information on scholarships for women is available in the booklet "Higher Education Opportunities for Minorities and Women" published by the U.S. Department of Education, Washington, D.C. 20202-5151. This booklet is updated yearly and, although designed primarily for minorities and women, many of the listings are for all students. Another good resource is the publication "Financial Aid: A Partial List of Resources for Women," available from the Project on the Status and Education of Women, Association of American Colleges, 1818 R Street, NW, Washington D.C. 20009.

# SO YOU WANT TO BE A DOCTOR? FREE MONEY FOR A CAREER IN THE HEALTH PROFESSIONS

If you are interested in pursuing a career in just about any area of medicine, whether it be as a doctor, nurse, chiropractor, therapist, veterinarian, or dentist, there is a scholarship or loan program available to you. Medical school is expensive,—very expensive, so looking for a way to help pay for a portion of your education is definitely worthwhile.

The federal government spends approximately $1.5 billion annually for the training of health professionals. Some of the money is earmarked for students, with the rest going to the schools to help offset the high cost of meeting the payroll of the medical training staff. Indirectly, this money does effect the students because it holds down tuition costs, which would be even higher if the school had to foot the entire payroll bill alone.

Students who apply for these scholarships should show a willingness to practice their professions in what is known as "shortage areas." These are predetermined areas within a specific field of medicine where the quality and availability of care is scarce and below the national average. The Department of Health and Human Services favors graduates who have shown a willingness to serve the communities in these "shortage" areas.

Some of the federal, individual and military medical and nursing programs that offer assistance include:

*National Health Service Corps Scholarships.* Apply through NHSCS, Rockville, MD). This is a competitive, support-for-service program for students of medicine, osteopathy, dentistry, and a limited number of other health-related disciplines. For each year of support, recipients must serve one year in full time clinical practice or in the employment of the National Health Service Corps working in an eligible manpower shortage area. For information write to: National Health Services Corps Scholarship Program, Room 17A31, 5600 Fishers Lane, Rockville, MD 20857.

*Health Education Assistance Loans* in medicine and dentistry, and osteopathic, optometric, podiatric and veterinary medicine (HEAL, Rockville, MD). They provide loans of up to $20,000 per year to a total of $80,000, with up to 25 years for repayment. These loans cannot be used for attending foreign medical institutions.

*Indian Health Service Scholarship.* Apply through the Indian Health Service (Rockville, MD). Pays all tuition and fees at schools of many health disciplines not included in the NHSCS. Same benefits and obligations as the National Health Service Corps Scholarship Program, with a minimum of two years in the Indian Health Service of the Health Services Administration or in practice in a shortage area serving an Indian population.

*Health Professions Student Loan.* Apply through your school. Uncle Sam will repay a good portion of this loan if the student chooses to practice in a shortage area. Covers tuition plus $2,500 per year.

*Nursing Student Loan Program.* These loans can be applied for through your school and are based on need. Loans up to $2,500 per year with a maximum of $10,000.

*Exceptional Need Scholarships.* Covers all tuition plus a monthly stipend. Good for one year only, but participants have priority for receiving NHSC Scholarship. Apply through your school.

*Commissioned Officer Student Training and Extern Program* (COSTEP). This is a work program. Undergraduates must have completed two years course study in a particular medical/science related field. Students must return to studies following completion of COSTEP program and serve as an extern in the medical facilities of the Public Health Service during school breaks of from 31 to 120 days. Recipients receive lieutenant's pay during this work period. There is no obligation of future service. Apply through COSTEP, Parklawn Bldg., 5600 Fishers Lane, Rockville, MD 20857.

Other programs:

*Rehabilitation Training.* Division of Resource Development, Rehabilitation Services Administration, Washington, D.C.

*Traineeships for Advanced Education of Professional Nurses.* Division of Nursing, Rockville, MD.

*Traineeships in Graduate Programs of Health Administration.* Division of Associated and Dental Health Professions, Rockville, MD.

*Mental Health Research.* Grants Management Branch, National Institute of Mental Health, Rockville, MD.

*Child Welfare Training Grants.* Children's Bureau, Washington, D.C.

*Occupational Safety and Health Training Grants.* Public Health Service, Rockville, MD.

*Psychiatric Nursing, Mental Health—Psychology, and Mental Health Sociology.* National Institute of Mental Health, Rockville, MD.

*American Medical Technologists Scholarship Program* (Park Ridge, IL) offers scholarships to high school graduates interested in pursuing medical technology or medical assistance careers.

Individual-based programs funded by private organizations are also available for specific career fields including blood technology, dental assistant, dental hygienist, dental lab technology, nursing, clinical laboratory, chiropractic, surgical technology, and several fields of therapy.

The military will pay for a medical or nursing education through the following programs:

*Uniformed Services University of the Health Sciences.* This is a school of medicine located in Bethesda, MD. Students receive lieutenant's pay in addition to expenses and all tuition fees.

*Armed Forces Health Professions Scholarship Program.* This program requires a service obligation, but pays for tuition, fees, books, lab expenses, and educational services plus a stipend. Five thousand awards per year in medicine and osteopathy (up to $8,200). A fact sheet is available from the Assistant Secretary of Defense (Health Affairs), The Pentagon, Washington, D.C.

*ROTC Nursing Program (Army and Air Force).* These are two-, three- or four-year scholarships that pay for tuition, textbooks, and fees plus a monthly stipend. A service obligation is also required. Write Army ROTC, Ft. Monroe, VA or Air Force ROTC, Maxwell AFB, AL.

*ROTC Pre-Health Professions Program (Air Force).* Scholarships for premedicine studies. Pays for tuition, books and fees, plus a monthly stipend. Also carries a service obligation. Write AFROTC, Maxwell AFB, AL.

## SCHOLARSHIPS FOR THE PHYSICALLY DISABLED

Below are four national programs that provide assistance to those students needing special help in meeting their extra budget requirements due to a handicap.

*The Alexander Graham Bell Association* for the Deaf (Washington, D.C.) gives awards between $500-$1,000 for students who are deaf and disabled.

*The Twitty, Milsap, Sterban Foundation* (Detroit, MI.), offers undergraduate and graduate scholarships in all fields of study to students who are partially sighted or blind. For information call: (313) 567-1920.

*The National Association for the Deaf* makes annual awards of $1,000 to graduate students studying in areas related to sign language or an aspect of the deaf community. For information contact: National Association of the Deaf, Stokoe Scholarship Secretary, 814 Thayer Ave., Silver Springs, MD 20910.

*The American Council of the Blind,* 1010 Vermont Ave., N.W., Suite 1100, Washington, D.C. 20005 offers annual scholarships of $1,000-$1,500.

Further information on special student aid is available through the Office of Vocational Rehabilitation of your state's Department of Education. You can also send for the free booklet, "Financial Aid for Students with Disabilities," HEATH, the National Clearing House on Postsecondary Education for Individuals with Handicaps, Suite 800, Washington, D.C., 20036. Or call the toll-free number for HEATH (Higher Education and Adult Training for People with Handicaps): (800) 544-3284.

## THE RHODES SCHOLARSHIP: REACH FOR THE SKY

Each year 32 American students with advanced undergraduate academic standing are selected as Rhodes Scholars to attend the University of Oxford in England. Requirements are very stringent, and candidates are evaluated on merit, without regard to race or gender. Selection is based on four criteria: scholarship, character, leadership, and physical vigor. Candidates must be U.S. citizens, unmarried, and between the ages of 18 and 23. Recipients of Rhodes Scholarships are entitled to a minimum of two years' study at the University. The Rhodes Scholarship is traditionally a very prestigious and coveted award.

For information on applying for a Rhodes Scholarship, contact the financial aid officer at your college or university or the Office of the American Secretary, Rhodes Scholarship Trust, Pomona College, Claremont, CA 91711.

# CHAPTER 3

# GRANTS: FREE MONEY BECAUSE YOU NEED IT

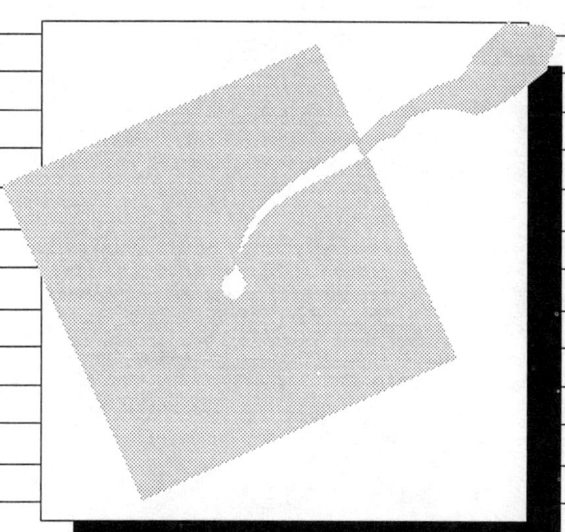

# GRANTS: FREE MONEY BECAUSE YOU NEED IT

Grants, like scholarships, are monetary awards given for educational purposes, that does not have to be paid back. In other words, grants are another source of free money to help finance your college education. Grants are generally awarded on the basis of need for one year only, with the recipient not having to show unusually exceptional abilities. Simply getting accepted by the college is normally sufficient academic achievement for grant consideration. This is what makes grants so desirable.

## THE PELL GRANT: UNCLE SAM'S REALLY BIG PROGRAM

The **Pell Grant** is the largest student aid program funded by the federal government. Nearly $4 billion a year is distributed under this federal program. For the academic year 1990-91, individual grants range from $200 to $2,300. The amount differs yearly depending on how much funding Congress gives the program.

Pell Grants are awarded to students solely on the basis of need for the purpose of continuing studies following high school graduation. Pell Grants are very desirable, as they are about the only outright gifts, with no strings attached, that one can receive from Uncle Sam. Also, Pell Grant awards are "student based," meaning the student receives the money directly or the school credits the award to the student's account.

In order to qualify for a Pell Grant, a student must attend school at least half-time and must be an undergraduate student without a bachelor's degree. Eligibility for a Pell Grant is determined by a standard formula developed by the U.S. Department of Education and passed into law by Congress. The formula, called the Pell Grant Methodology, produces a Pell Grant Index (PGI) number, formerly called Student Aid Index. Your Student Aid Report (SAR), the report you receive after you apply for federal aid, shows your PGI number. If you are using a form other than the federal AFSA form (such as the FFS or FAF form), you will need to check the box provided near the end of the form if you want to be considered for federal student aid.

The PGI number is very important in the financial aid analysis process. It is the number that tells whether you may be able to get a Pell Grant. If you are eligible for a Pell Grant, your school will use this number to determine the amount of your award. The formula used to determine the PGI is described in detail in a guidebook that is available by writing:

FORMULA BOOK (Pell Grant)
Department L-10,
Pueblo, CO 81009-0015.

The Student Aid Report also gives you your Family Contribution (FC) number, which is then used in determining eligibility for campus-based and Stafford Loan programs. This number is also used to determine the amount of your grant, loan, or work/study award. The higher the family contribution, the less likely a Pell Grant will be given, since it is a need-based program, the purpose of which is to make sure that all eligible students have at least some of the money they need to continue their education. If a family contribution exceeds approximately $2,100, you probably won't qualify for a Pell Grant. However, logical or not, you won't be considered for other awards unless you have been turned down for a Pell.

If your SAR says you are eligible for a Pell Grant, it will have three parts (if you are not eligible, the SAR will have only two parts):

Part 1 is an Information Summary.

Part 2 is an Information Review Form, which is used to correct or change any information on the SAR that is incorrect.

Part 3 is the Pell Grant Payment Document to be used by your school.

If all the information on the SAR is correct, you need to sign it and send photocopies to the financial aid administrator of each school where an application is being made. (Once you decide on which school to attend, the financial aid administrator at that school will use the information on the SAR to determine the amount of the Pell Grant award.)

An interesting fact is that about one third of the more than 5.5 million applications received for Pell Grants are returned for validation of information or for leaving out critical information necessary to complete the form. This occurs when the person analyzing the application suspects something "fishy," such as unsubstantiated statements that are essential to determining need. If you are selected by the Department of Education or your school for the "verification" process, you may be asked to prove information such as:

- Income.
- Federal income tax paid.
- Size of household.
- Number of family members enrolled in postsecondary education at least half-time.
- Certain untaxed income and benefits.
- Social Security benefits.
- Child support.

The financial aid administrator can require you to produce certain documents or other information, including a Verification Worksheet, a copy of the most recent signed U.S. income tax return (yours and/or your parents), W-2 Forms or statements from agencies such as the Social Security or Veterans Administration. If you don't provide the proof requested, you may not receive federal aid or aid from other sources.

It is important that every student considering financial aid apply for a Pell Grant, even if he/she believes he is going to be rejected. As mentioned above, these grants provide the foundation, the bottom layer upon which other forms of financial aid awards are based. The Pell Grant application is also a prerequisite for a Guaranteed Student Loan.

Finally, although the deadline for filing a student aid application is May 1, you should apply as soon as possible after January 1 of the year you plan to attend college. Other aid programs may have deadlines earlier than May 1, so *always* check with the financial aid administrator at your school about filing deadlines. The sooner you apply, the better. If you don't apply early for campus-based programs, you may miss out on these limited funds.

## SUPPLEMENTAL EDUCATIONAL OPPORTUNITY GRANTS (SEOG)

This is a college based program, meaning the participating college receives from the federal government a set amount of funds to distribute. Although SEOGs are designed to supplement other sources of financial aid for students who qualify for additional assistance, there is no guarantee that a school will receive enough money to award all eligible students. Therefore, SEOGs are very competitive and desirable. It is important that students apply for a SEOG early (check with your school for the deadline) so as not to lose their chance for these funds. Grants range from $100 up to $4,000 per year to individual students.

Some colleges may award SEOGs to students who are enrolled on a less than half-time basis. How much aid you receive is dependent on your financial need (which generally must be exceptional) and other financial aid you will be receiving. Receivers of Pell Grants are given first priority in the awarding of SEOG grants. As with other grants, the money does not have to be repaid.

If you receive a SEOG, your school will credit the funds to your account, pay you directly or use a combination of these methods. Students must be paid at least once per term, or if traditional terms (semester, trimester, quarters) are not used, they must be paid by the school at least twice during the academic year.

## STATE GRANTS

Most states have grant programs, which vary from state to state. Again, the primary criterion is *generally* need, which determines the amount of the grant. For students meeting the need requirements, certain academic standards may also be necessary, such as ranking in the top 25 percent of their high school class. For states using merit as a primary criterion, academic requirements may be even higher. The maximum award is about $2,000. Most states provide special assistance to students attending private colleges and some even provide funds to residents attending schools out-of-state. An example of a state grant program is the Illinois Monetary Award Program.

There are some merit-based state programs based solely on academic excellence. These programs are on the rise as colleges compete to keep their best students within their state educational system.

California, Illinois, New Jersey, New York, Minnesota, and Pennsylvania make the most awards of any states. Virginia and Texas each have unique programs for special incentive grants, whereby students of one racial group are encouraged to attend a state public college or university in which another racial group makes up a significant proportion of the student body.

For information on individual state programs, contact the student aid agency in your state. Your high school college counselor, college financial aid officer, or library should have the address and telephone number.

## TUITION EQUALIZATION GRANTS

These are programs designed to reduce the differences in tuition costs between public schools and private colleges. Nearly $100 million worth of tuition equalization grants are awarded by states including Alabama, Florida, Georgia, North Carolina, Ohio, and Virginia. Some private colleges will also have their own form of a tuition equalization program in order to attract students from public schools. Certain academic standards are usually required with the granting of tuition funds.

## OTHER SOURCES OF GRANT MONEY

Like scholarships, there are many individual grant programs funded by private foundations, individual institutions, special membership groups, and organizations. A few examples appear on the following page.

*University Laboratory Cooperative Program* (Office of Energy Research, Department of Energy, Washington, D.C.) will provide science, engineering, or technology undergraduates special energy training and research-related work experience in energy research.

*Young Scholars Program of the National Endowment for the Humanities* awards grants from $1,800 to $2,000 for a period of four months for projects in history, mathematics, languages, or literature.

*Bureau of Indian Affairs* (BIA) grants, also known as Native American grants, are awarded to descendants of Native Americans (Indians) or Native Alaskans belonging to a tribe recognized by the U.S. Bureau of Indian Affairs. Tuition and stipends are paid to students who have established financial need.

*The Abelard Foundation* (New York, NY) grants awards from $500 to $5,000 to underprivileged and minority students in the areas of health, social welfare, humanities, arts, and education.

Finally, do not overlook the possibility of receiving a grant from your school. Many schools offer creative, innovative assistance plans to aid bright, promising students who are seeking additional help. Alumni clubs and organizations are often overlooked as a potential source of aid. Another is asking for a multifamily discount if you have siblings (or other family members) attending college with you at the same time. Some schools will pay a portion (or sometimes even all) of a student's tuition if his family has suffered extreme financial hardships, i.e., students whose parents have lost their farms in the latest agricultural/farming crisis or students with unemployed parents. If you are a senior citizen, some schools will give you a 50 percent or higher discount on fees and tuition. If you are an up and coming student leader, editor of a school publication, or officer of the student government, you might be eligible for a significant tuition discount. Community service, public service, or being an active volunteer may earn you special dispensation when it comes to paying for school. If you believe you possess special circumstances or constitute a unique case for consideration of a tuition/fee grant, discuss your situation with your financial aid officer, department head, trusted coach, or professor. They may be able to work something out for you.

# CHAPTER
# 4
# EARN AND LEARN: WORK/STUDY PROGRAMS

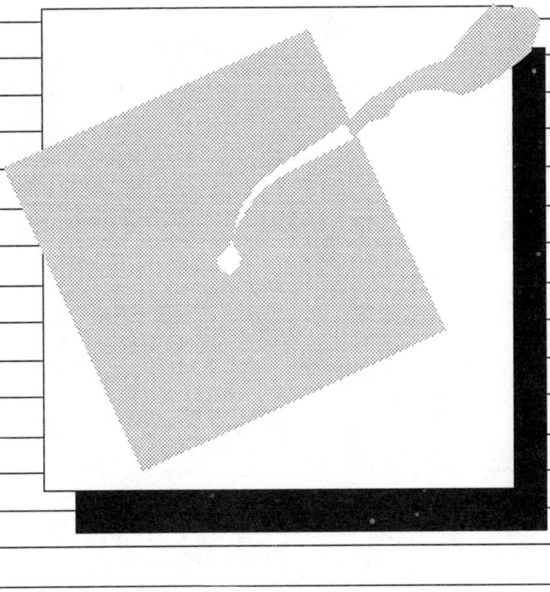

# EARN AND LEARN: WORK/STUDY PROGRAMS

Although these are not technically programs that award or offer free money, they are often an important component in a financial aid package, and certainly are an important means of reducing your college costs. If the "need" portion of your student budget is not met through grants and scholarships, a work/study program may be included to make up the remaining need.

Some alternative "earn and learn" programs will be mentioned in the upcoming chapter on "More Money Saving Options." This chapter explains the "official" work/study programs offered by colleges and funded by the federal government.

These "campus based" programs are awarded on the basis of need. The main purpose of a College Work Study (CWS) program is to help achieve the goal of lowering college costs. CWS programs give students the chance to earn money to help pay their educational expenses. They are more desirable than loans since there is no financial obligation involved in College Work/Study programs.

A hidden benefit of a CWS program is that students enrolled in the programs often learn to budget their time better and manage their money more efficiently and wisely.

Jobs in a work/study program are generally assigned on-campus rather than off-campus. Most students work between 10 and 15 hours a week in various jobs such as library assistant, cafeteria/dining room worker, office assistant, maintenance and grounds keeping, faculty aide, and other similar positions. A student must be enrolled at least half-time in order to qualify for the program.

If a student works off-campus, it must be for a public or private nonprofit organization or a federal, state, or local public organization. In some cases schools have agreements with private sector employers for CWS jobs. Off-campus employers are subsidized by the federal government.

Students are paid at least the current federal hourly minimum wage. The amount a student can earn is determined and limited by (1) the student's financial need; (2) how much money is being funded to his/her school for the CWS program; and (3) other financial aid the student is receiving. The amount earned by a student can never exceed the total CWS award. If you are awarded CWS as part of your aid package, your school's financial aid officer works with you to set up your work schedule in accordance with your class schedule, health, and academic progress.

CWS programs are very much in demand at colleges, and since each school is allocated only a certain amount of funds, it is important to apply early to enroll in this popular, competitive program.

# CHAPTER
# 5
# LOANS: WHAT YOU'LL NEED TO FILL IN THE BLANKS

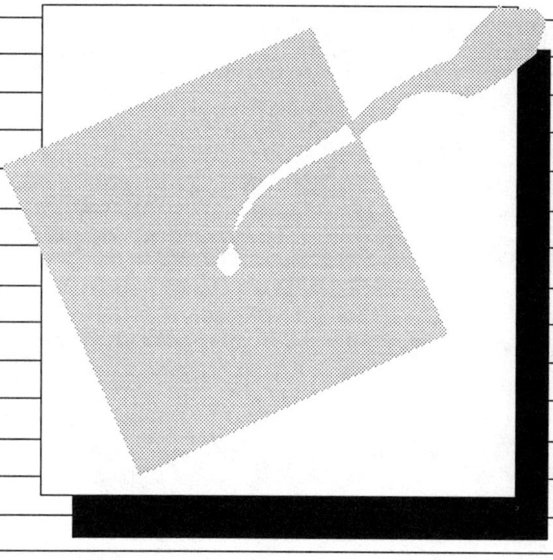

# LOANS: WHAT YOU'LL NEED TO FILL IN THE BLANKS

On the scale of desirability for financial aid, loans are in last place following grants, scholarships, and work/study programs, since money from loans has to be paid back. There are many loan programs with varying rates of interest and pay-back plans, but aside from a limited number of exceptions, the money is not "free." However, we have included this section in our book since it may be necessary for some students to make up a portion of their financial aid package with one or more loans after the free money avenues have been exhausted. In this chapter we briefly describe some of the more well-known programs and a few lesser- known innovative ones.

An important note: Students cannot borrow more than the cost of education at their school, minus any other financial aid being received. Also, if the student fails to repay back the loan, he/she runs the risk of going into default, in which case the entire amount may be demanded, and the student's future credit rating may be seriously affected.

## PERKINS LOAN

The Perkins Loan Program is a federal campus-based program administered by colleges and universities. The Perkins Loan carries the lowest interest rate of any educational loan, 5 percent, making it one of the most desirable. The criteria for selection include need (usually exceptional) and availability of funds at the student's college, as well as the amount of other aid the student is getting.

Students can borrow up to $4,500 in the first two years of college leading to a bachelor's degree, or up to $9,000 between the third year and graduation (includes any amount previously borrowed under Perkins loan in the first two years).

Recipients of a Perkins loan sign a promissory note agreeing to repay the loan. Repayment of the loan begins nine months after a student graduates, leaves school, or drops below the half-time attendance level. The loan must be completely paid within 10 years. There are payment plans that allow borrowers to spread their payments over the 10-year period. However, if a student defaults on his loan, the school can require repayment of the entire amount immediately, including all interest, collection, and late-payment charges. The school can also sue the student to collect its money and can ask the federal government for help in collecting it. As we warned above, the school or federal government will also notify credit bureaus of the default, which may affect future credit rating.

Deferments of payments after a student has left school are possible, as long as the loan is not in default. A deferment must be applied for through the school. In a few special circumstances, all or part of a Perkins Loan can be canceled or postponed, i.e., if the student dies or is permanently disabled, becomes a full-time teacher of handicapped or low-income children, works in a Head Start program, serves as a Peace Corps or VISTA volunteer, or serves as an enlisted person in a specialty in one of the armed forces.

## STAFFORD LOAN (formerly Guaranteed Student Loan Program)

Stafford Loans are low-interest loans made to students attending school at least half-time. The loans are made by a lender such as a bank, credit union, or savings and loan association. Sometimes the school makes the loan.

The reason this was called the Guaranteed Student Loan Program in the past is because the loans are insured by the guarantee agency in each state and reinsured by the federal government. This program is now the major source of credit for educational loans.

Because the loans are subsidized by the government, the interest rate is lower than most commercially available loans. For the first four years of repayment the interest rate is 8 percent, and 10 percent thereafter. There is also an "origination fee" of 5 percent, which helps the government reduce its cost of subsidizing the loan. Repayment of both principal and interest are deferred until six months after graduation or the student leaves school. The loan must be paid within 5 to 10 years.

Eligibility for a Stafford Loan is based on demonstrated need. Freshmen and sophomores can borrow up to $2,625 per year; juniors and seniors up to $4,000 per year. The maximum amount an undergraduate may borrow is $17,250.

As with the Perkins Loan, a Stafford Loan can be repaid through a schedule of monthly payments with amounts depending on the length of the repayment period. Default will also result in collection of the entire amount and the possibility of a damaged credit rating in the future. In a few cases the loan can be deferred or canceled. To find out who the lenders are in your State, you can contact the State guarantee agency (see Appendix II through this program). More information about borrowing is available through the Federal Student Aid Information Center's toll-free hotline: (800) 333-INFO.

## PLUS/SLS LOANS

Parents Loans to Undergraduate Students (PLUS) are loans for parents who want to borrow to help pay for their children's education. Supplemental Loans for Students (SLS) are for student borrowers. These loans are not based on need. Like the Stafford Loans, the money is funded by a lender such as a bank, credit union, or S&L association.

Parents may borrow up to $4,000 per year, to a total of $20,000, for each child who is enrolled at least half-time and is a dependent student. For independent students, SLS loans are available for the same amounts. This does not include money borrowed in the Stafford Loan program.

Note: Students must apply for both a Pell Grant and a Stafford Loan before they can be considered eligible for an SLS. If found eligible for aid from either or both of these programs, the amount you can borrow under SLS may be affected by the amount of aid awarded from other sources.

Loans are made for up to 10 years and carry a variable annual interest rate, keyed into the previous year's average 91-day Treasury bill rate with a cap of 12 percent. A lender may also charge an insurance premium of up to 3 percent of the loan principal. Repayment of both interest and principal generally must begin within 60 days after the last loan disbursement. Again, there are a few special cases where deferment or cancellation of a loan may be granted.

Warning: A student's eligibility for any federal loan program or a Pell Grant can be suspended or terminated by a court as part of a conviction for possessing or distributing drugs.

## LOAN CONSOLIDATION

If you have taken out more than one loan to finance your education, *loan consolidation* makes it possible to pay them all back using one repayment plan. (PLUS loans are not eligible for consolidation.) A loan consolidation program is available to students having loans totaling at least $5,000. Before loans can be consolidated, the student must be in repayment or in the grace period between graduation and repayment.

Loan consolidation allows eligible lenders to pay off existing student loans and create one new loan. Under consolidation a student can stretch repayment up to a maximum of 25 years, with smaller monthly payments, depending on the total amount to be repaid. Interest on the new loan will be 9 percent or more, depending on interest rates of the loans consolidated.

## OTHER LOAN PROGRAMS

Many schools offer innovative and low-interest loans to students and their parents. Some colleges now offer adjustable-rate tuition loans. An example is the University of Pennsylvania. Monthly payments stay the same, but interest rates and tuition costs fluctuate accordingly.

An unusual approach is the "moral obligation" scholarship program in which students receive funds that carry a moral, but not a legal, repayment obligation. Since there is no legal obligation to repay the loan, the payments made to the college can be claimed as tax-deductible gifts by the former student. For example, the HELP program at

Lafayette College makes loans to qualified parents up to $5,000 and will fully subsidize the interest while the student is enrolled, with repayment on the principal deferred until after graduation.

There are also cases where the school will allow a student to use outside scholarship awards to replace the loan portion of a financial aid package. There are also special scholarships and loans at some schools earmarked for "middle income families." Another creative program at some schools rewards students for community service. These schools award scholarships or repay up to 100 percent of student loans for spending time in community service, tutoring, volunteer work, or teaching nonreaders to read. For example, The University of California at Berkeley rewards students by repaying their federal loans if they choose careers in public or community service after graduation.

Some banks, credit unions, investment firms and other organizations have created special educational loan programs with more favorable interest rates or other features that make the loans more attractive. For example, the Alliance Education Loan Program at the Bank of Boston will lend money to credit worthy undergraduates attending accredited colleges and universities. The Consortium on Financing Higher Education, a group of 30 high-cost, selective, primarily East Coast schools, has a supplemental loan program for parents (SHARE). Parents can borrow up to $20,000 per year and take up to 20 years to repay. The Massachusetts Education Loan Authority (MELA) lets students and parents borrow up to 100 percent of the costs for college at 43 different schools on a 15-year fixed interest rate basis.

Some states offer loans separate from government authorized loans. Alaska offers a very generous program after fulfillment of a two-year residency requirement. Minnesota and Maine both offer loan programs with interest rates tied into T-bill rates and the prime lending rate. Money for state loans is usually secured through tax-exempt bond issues or an authorized nonprofit state agency.

One of the most interesting programs being conducted at both state and national levels provides tuition aid to prospective teachers in return for services. These programs qualify for our free money status because they provide "forgivable loans" as rewards for easing the teacher shortage crisis. The state of Florida is one example of many states that practically pay for students to go to teachers' colleges. The state agrees to forgive the student's loans if the student agrees to teach a certain number of years in Florida after graduation. Naturally, if the student doesn't go into teaching, the loan must be repaid.

The Paul Douglas Teacher Scholarship Program, while technically a scholarship program, awards outstanding high school graduates who want to pursue teaching careers. Students who graduate in the top 10 percent of their high school class are eligible for awards up to $5,000. The recipients are generally required to teach two years for each year of scholarship assistance. Over 10,000 awards are given yearly in this state-administered program.

It is predicted that within the next few years similar programs will be offered in various fields including law enforcement and police work, that can be stimulated by educational gifts.

## PRIVATE LOAN SOURCES

As with scholarships and grants, many private organizations and affiliated groups, businesses, unions, foundations, etc., give special interest or general educational loans to qualifying students. A few noteworthy ones include:

> *The Hattie M. Strong Foundation*, which grants interest free loans up to $2,500 to college students with one year or less remaining before graduation.
>
> *The Loan Fund for Women in Engineering Studies* given by the Business and Professional Women's (BPW) Foundation.
>
> *The United Methodist Church Student Loans* given for general studies to eligible members from all minority groups.
>
> *The Pickett & Hatcher Educational Fund*, which gives loans with preference to liberal arts majors meeting specific criteria in scholastic ability, financial need, and character.
>
> *The Knights Templar Educational Foundation,* which awards between $3,000 and $6,000 to qualifying students in their last two years of college.

Look in Appendix III of this book for sources to locate these private funds.

# A FINAL WORD ON LOANS

In addition to the loans described in the preceding pages, there are many other innovative aid programs, loan payment plans, and tuition payment packages available through individual schools. The only way to find out if one of these plans exists at your school, or possibly create a new one for yourself, is to ask. All schools receive funds for student aid in one form or another. They are also in fierce competition with each other to keep their best and brightest students and continue to attract those kinds of students in the future. The more you ask about ways to help finance your education, the more you will find out about unusual avenues and alternative possibilities that may be just what you need to get that degree.

# CHAPTER 6
# "JOIN UP" AND GO TO COLLEGE FOR FREE

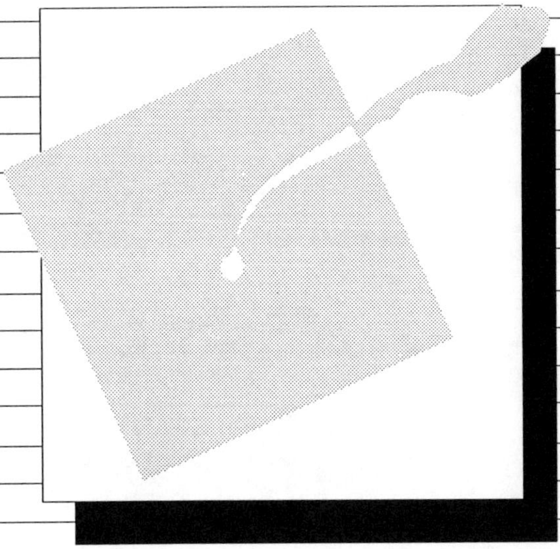

# "JOIN UP" AND GO TO COLLEGE FOR FREE

The armed forces offer some of the most extraordinary savings available in earning a full college degree. In fact, in their effort to educate our nation's uniformed personnel, they will actually pay you to go to college. Funds for a college education can be used before entering the service, while in service, or after discharge. More than $1 billion a year is given to qualified students, either as payment for training or as a reward for service. If either one or both of your parents have served in the military, you may be eligible for financial aid (see Chapter 3 for scholarships).

With few exceptions, federal aid programs exist exclusively for students with need. The *big* exceptions are the military programs and veteran benefits, which are funded without reference to need. Rich or poor, male or female, a student who qualifies for a program has a chance of tapping into this huge source of dollars.

Getting money for tuition, however, is going to be more work than just a quick salute. The armed forces have their own goals, which are to train career officers and specialists to serve in their particular branch.

## MILITARY ACADEMIES

All five U.S. service academies offer scholarships at essentially no cost to the student. These academies are the U.S. Air Force Academy, the U.S. Military Academy, the U.S. Naval Academy, The U.S. Coast Guard Academy, and the U.S. Merchant Marine Academy.

The academies are extremely competitive and have stringent requirements for acceptance. Students must meet strict health and physical demands; academic records and test scores must exceed those of other applicants; you must be between the ages of 17 and 21, never married, a U.S. citizen, and you must have a clean record. Extracurricular activities and leadership qualities are also considered. In addition, an applicant must be nominated by an elected official, i.e., a U.S. Congressman or Senator (the Coast Guard is the one exception).

However, once a student is accepted, they can expect to receive free tuition and fees, free room and board, books and supplies, and a monthly stipend or salary for miscellaneous expenses. In other words, a free college education.

## ROTC PROGRAMS

The Reserve Officer Training Corps (ROTC) offers two-, three-, four- and five-year scholarship programs and a regular four-year program. The Air Force, Army, Navy, and Marines all offer ROTC programs. These programs are available for men and women between the ages of 17 and 25 and, like the academies, have strict physical and academic requirements. The competition is fairly stiff, but students have the choice of more than 600 university and college campuses from which to chose.

The ROTC scholarship programs cover tuition, books, and fees, as well as a $100 tax-free monthly allowance. (The Army pays up to $7,000 or 80 percent, whichever is higher, annually, for its four-year scholarship.) Payment for room, board, transportation, and miscellaneous expenses, depends on the ROTC scholarship policies at individual schools. The ROTC regular four-year program pays a tax-free subsistence allowance of $100 a month following a student's freshman and sophomore years in the program.

While attending college, students must enlist in the Army, Navy, or Air Force. They are also required to accept an officer commission upon graduation and enlist for up to eight years (depending on the branch of service) in the reserves (including active duty) immediately after graduation.

The ROTC also offers a limited number of Army scholarships to applicants who agree to attend an Historically Black College. Students awarded scholarships through this Quality Enrichment Program (QEP) are required to attend an Historically Black College for the duration of their scholarship. Included in these colleges are:

ALABAMA A&M UNIVERSITY
Normal, Alabama

TUSKEGEE INSTITUTE
Tuskegee, Alabama

UNIVERSITY OF ARKANSAS AT PINE BLUFF
Pine Bluff, Arkansas

HOWARD UNIVERSITY
Washington, D.C.

FLORIDA A&M UNIVERSITY
Tallahassee, Florida

FORT VALLEY STATE COLLEGE
Ft. Valley, Georgia

SOUTHERN UNIVERSITY and A&M COLLEGE
Baton Rouge, Louisiana

MORGAN STATE UNIVERSITY
Baltimore, Maryland

JACKSON STATE UNIVERSITY
Jackson, Michigan

LINCOLN UNIVERSITY
Jefferson City, Missouri

NORTH CAROLINA A&T STATE UNIVERSITY
Greensboro, North Carolina

ST. AUGUSTINE'S COLLEGE
Raleigh, North Carolina

CENTRAL STATE UNIVERSITY
Wilberforce, Ohio

SOUTH CAROLINA STATE COLLEGE
Orangeburn, South Carolina

PRAIRIE VIEW A&M COLLEGE
Prairie View, Texas

HAMPTON UNIVERSITY
Hampton, Virginia

NORFOLK STATE UNIVERSITY
Norfolk, Virginia

VIRGINIA STATE UNIVERSITY
Petersburg, Virginia

WEST VIRGINIA STATE COLLEGE
Institute, West Virginia

## ATTENDING COLLEGE WHILE IN SERVICE

There are excellent advantages for getting a college degree while serving in the military, mainly the low costs and practical experience gained.

"In-service" education is encouraged by all branches of the armed forces. The service will pick up most of the tuition costs while the enlisted service person attends classes at a campus near the military base.

An example of an in-service program is funded through the new GI Bill where a service member and the government work together to build an education savings account. Allocations are taken from the enlisted persons paycheck (not exceeding a total of $1,200) while he or she is on active duty. The government matches these deposits (sometimes as much as $8 for every $1). This can add up to a sizable amount during an enlistment.

Cash bonuses for enlistment in the reserves and for completing advance training are also among the benefits available while in service. The Army Reserve, National Guard, and the regular Army also offer repayment on federal student loans as incentive for enlistment in selected skills.

## POSTSERVICE BENEFITS

The new GI Bill, as explained above, works as a contributory system. While on active duty, the government helps build up the enlisted person's educational savings account. The Veterans Administration will also contribute funds to help. Additional bonuses are awarded for special services and training. A soldier, sailor, or airman can attend college full-time after active duty with the accumulated moneys being paid out to him in monthly installments.

The new GI Bill affects everyone enlisting after July 1, 1985. The VEAP (Veteran's Educational Assistance Program) provides educational benefits for those enlisted prior to that date. It is similar to the new GI Bill in that the government matches participants' contributions (two to one up to $5,400).

Dependents of deceased or disabled veterans as well dependents of POWs and MIAs are eligible for Social Security Administration and Veterans Administration educational benefits.

Immediate family members of veterans can apply for college education aid programs including special scholarships ( EX. AMVETS National Scholarship Program) and interest-free loans.

For a complete listing of association benefits and programs available to families of former military members write for the annual guide: "Need a Lift?," $2, published by the American Legion, Emblem Sales, P.O. Box 1050, Indianapolis, IN 46206.

Another recommended source for exploring military related opportunities for financial aid is *How the Military Will Help You Pay for College,* by Don M. Betterton (see Appendix III).

## OTHER MILITARY PROGRAMS

The Defense Activity for Non-Traditional Education Support (DANTE) is a program of correspondence courses that permits enlisted personnel to earn college credit and advance toward qualifying for college admission. Several hundred courses (high school through postgraduate level) are offered as well as tests that establish job proficiency in certain skills and help enlistees earn high school diplomas.

The Service Members Opportunity College Program (SOC) is a flexible academic program with colleges set up to suit the individual lifestyles of service members. These programs are offered by the Army, Navy, Air Force, Marine Corps and Coast Guard, whose program is the most generous—paying up to 100 percent of tuition costs.

There are also programs that offer substantial aid for students interested in a career as a health professional. A pre-med student can apply for an Armed Forces Health Professions Scholarship while a senior. A scholarship will pay tuition, fees, and books plus a generous monthly allowance. There is a military obligation after graduation from medical school of one year of service for each year of the scholarship (see Chapter 3).

The ROTC offers two-three- and four-year scholarships in their Nursing Programs in both the Army and Air Force. Students attending an approved nursing school while enrolled with a ROTC unit receive payment for tuition, textbooks, and fees, plus a monthly stipend (up to $7,800 a year or 80 percent of tuition, whichever is larger).

The Uniformed Services University of the Health Sciences in Bethesda, Maryland, is a School of Medicine that pays its students as active duty military officers, plus tuition and expenses. Most of the students have prior military associations, although those with none are trained as officers while attending medical school. Service in the military branch in which they were trained is required after graduation.

The new G.I. Bill also has a provision that permits a service to add dollars to the benefits for men and women who enlist. The army's "New Army College Fund" has done this to fill combat assignments and attract recruits in the technical fields. Men and women serving in the active reserves can receive benefits from the new GI Bill in return for a long term re-enlistment. For more information on "The New Army College Incentive" call toll-free (800) USA-ARMY.

# CHAPTER 7
# MORE MONEY SAVING OPTIONS

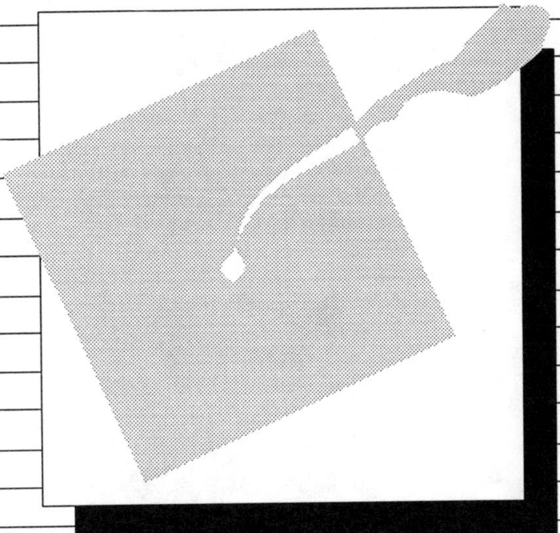

# MORE MONEY SAVING OPTIONS

In addition to what we have discussed thus far, there are other alternative routes to actually getting free money for a college education. These are the nonconventional, nonloan, nonwork/study, nonaward options of saving money, earning money, and sometimes redistributing money in unique ways in order to make the bite of college less painful. There are some plans that can be put into effect shortly before entering college and those that require several years of planning ahead. We have broken these options into two categories, one for students and one for parents, depending on who is actually responsible for footing the bills (sometimes it takes a cooperative family effort to be successful).

These are viable, creative strategies, which sometimes take a lot of work and fortitude on a student's part and long-range planning for parents. But again, they serve to ease the financial burden when it suddenly hits you.

## WAYS TO SAVE IF YOU'RE A STUDENT

***Accelerated Degree.*** If a student takes on a heavier than usual course schedule, attends summer school, fulfills as many requirements for graduation as possible, he or she can earn a bachelor's degree in three years instead of the traditional four. This is a special program that can be arranged with the college admissions office. It saves a year's worth of costs and tuition.

***Co-operative Education.*** In this program, which is usually referred to as a "co-op," the student alternates formal study in the classroom with work experience in the declared major. Often times, most college expenses can be covered with this arrangement. The program is run by the individual college, with more than 900 colleges and 50,000 employers participating.

There are three methods in which a student can go "co-op": (1) alternating semesters of being a full-time student and a full-time employee; (2) working full-time during the day and going to classes in the evening; or (3) attending classes part-time and working part-time, usually 15 to 25 hours a week.

Although choosing a "co-op" education takes more time to earn a degree, there are several advantages and benefits. The most obvious is that students earn money that pays for the education they are simultaneously receiving. Also, actual work experience in their chosen field often puts them ahead of some of their contemporaries who have less on-the-job experience when they graduate. Many companies reward their "co-op" workers with a promotion upon graduation. Another benefit is that actual hands-on experience can often make classwork easier for those courses being taking within a student's major.

For more information write for The Co-Op Education Undergraduate Program Directory, The National Commission for Cooperative Education, 360 Huntington Avenue, Boston, MA 02115.

***Off-Campus Living.*** If a college allows its students to live off campus in noncollege housing, there are a lot of cost reductions that can be made. Generally, the cheapest way to go is to commute from your parents' home. These students are usually referred to in college catalogs as "commuters." Even though Mom and Dad are still paying for food for meals, there are big savings in rent, utilities, maintenance, etc. Most colleges with their own housing (provided in dorms on campus or off-campus college owned housing) charge a set fee for room and board, which includes a specific number of meals per week (usually between 14 and 21). This charge is built into the student's expense budget.

If, however, a student lives off-campus in private housing with several students sharing an apartment, or other private housing, he or she can usually economize on certain expenses (i.e., living off pizza and fast food for nine months, carpooling, sharing costs of books and supplies) that eat into the total yearly budget.

Information about student expense budgets, estimates and comparisons between "resident" and "commuter" costs can be found in current college catalogs.

***Junior Fellowships.*** This program is sponsored by Uncle Sam for students with financial need who place within the upper 10 percent of their high school graduating class. Junior Fellowships is a job placement program that provides opportunities to work for a federal agency during academic breaks. Students are often offered their jobs on a full-time basis or receive a promotion within the agency when they graduate. Five thousand scholarships are offered in this program, which often has several thousand vacancies because of poor promotion and advertising. Checking into this national program is worthwhile since competition is not as fierce as other oversubscribed programs.

***Internships.*** Approximately 1.5 million college students participate yearly in internships. An internship program is a carefully monitored and planned work or service experience where the student has an international learning goal. This goal is actively reflected and maintained throughout the internship and extends through the students college career, rather than just during academic breaks. Interns may or may not receive the pay, but nearly always receive practical experience. This is important to liberal arts majors, because there are a limited number of co-op jobs available to them. Interns generally get paid between $75 and $100 per week, not a great deal, but enough to cover some expenses. Both profit and non-profit organizations participate in these creative programs.

For more information write: National Society for Internships and Experiential Education, 3509 Haworth Dr. #207, Raleigh, NC 27609-7229.

***Advanced Placement Program.*** This program can reduce the overall cost of an education by reducing the length of time involved in earning a degree (similar to the accelerated program). If a student can demonstrate a proficiency in college-level studies through exams sponsored by the College Board or the American College Testing Program and accepted by the Advanced Placement Program, then he/she can enter college at the sophomore level. Sometimes prior independent study or "life experience" can qualify a student for advanced placement.

Even if a student is not looking to save a year's college costs and enter as a sophomore, taking APP courses in high school impresses the college admissions office and enhances the student's chances of admission. There are over 200 colleges and universities participating in the APP Program. For example, for several years, Harvard has admitted approximately 10 percent of each entering class as sophomores largely on the basis of APP scores. That alone can save a student more than $18,000 in tuition and housing!

For more information send for the free booklet: "A Guide to the Advanced Placement Program," Advanced Placement, P.O. Box 6671, Princeton, NJ 08541.

***External Degree Program.*** This is one of the lowest-cost programs for getting a degree, and it can be achieved without ever setting a foot in the classroom! Two states sponsoring these degrees are New Jersey, from the Thomas A. Edison State College, and New York, in a state program called Regents External Degree Program. All credits earned from approved sources are applied toward a bachelor's or associate degree. These are "study at home" and correspondence type courses.

Earning this type of degree has the advantage of giving students lots of flexibility in their lifestyle since no attendance is required. Costs are very low, and the entire degree can be awarded through the examination process, although it takes a lot of initiative, determination, and discipline. Also, college credit already earned through conventional class attendance is taken into consideration. Students having attended several colleges can transfer all their credits to the institution sponsoring the external degree, thereby consolidating their studies and completing them with whatever credits are remaining. Degree credits for cultural experience or work, specialized skills, or areas of knowledge are also given.

There are several public and private colleges that offer external degree programs, some requiring no actual attendance on campus and others requiring varying degrees (approximately 25 percent) of the credit earned from on-campus attendance. These degrees are very attractive to older students who have accumulated a great deal of life experience and knowledge since graduating high school.

Some private colleges advertise their programs in the classified sections of business magazines. Before enrolling in any program, always check the credibility of the institution, either through the Better Business Bureau, Chamber of Commerce, or your state's department of education.

Finally, public television offers a nontraditional avenue for receiving college credit, at no cost (or minimal cost for cable subscribers). Over 1,500 colleges accept telecourses for credit, but these programs must be accredited by the college in order to count towards a degree. The Public Broadcasting System's Adult Learning Service has a very wide-based program. Also, courses offered by Mind Extension University are accepted at several state universities. They can be reached by calling 1-800-MIND.

***In-State Attendance.*** Most public schools have different fee schedules for in-state and out-of-state students. The fees for students coming from out-of-state can be several thousand dollars more than for students who are in-state residents. One way a student can get around the out-of-state residency charge is to buy property near the campus, live in it (establishing residency), rent out empty rooms if it is large enough, and sell it following graduation (hopefully at a profit).

**EXAMPLES OF IN-STATE AND OUT-OF-STATE STUDENT FEES**

| Name Of School | In-State Fees | Out-of-State Fees |
|---|---|---|
| Calif. State Univ.—Fresno | $ 844 | $5,670 |
| Calif. State Univ.—Long Beach | 820 | 5,670 |
| San Diego State University | 846 | 5,670 |
| Univ. of Calif.—Berkeley | 1,672 | 7,472 |
| Univ. of Calif.—Los Angeles | 1,533 | 7,332 |

# WAYS TO SAVE FOR PARENTS

The options for parents come in many different sizes, shapes, and packages. Some are long-range savings plans that can be started when a child is born. Some go into effect when the child enters college and continue until graduation. And some are designed to shift income to both save on taxes in the long term and help make the "family contribution" portion of a financial aid application smaller, thus increasing chances for a greater loan/aid program being developed. The goal of increasing a middle income family's chances for financial aid eligibility must be taken seriously. Repositioning assets and reducing the adjusted gross income are two important ways for achieving this goal.

Chart 13
**Monthly Investment Needed to Meet the Projected Costs of College**

| When your child will begin college | 1991 | 1994 | 1997 | 2000 | 2003 | 2006 | 2009 |
|---|---|---|---|---|---|---|---|
| | This year | in 3 years | in 6 years | in 9 years | in 12 years | in 15 years | in 18 years |
| 4-year public college - monthly savings necessary | $2,228 | $783 | $423 | $303 | $243 | $207 | $183 |
| 4-year private college - monthly savings necessary | $4,724 | $1,661 | $896 | $642 | $515 | $438 | $387 |

*Assumes 8 percent annual pretax return on investment.

***Tuition Prepayment Plans, Tuition Futures, and Guaranteed Tuition Plans.*** There are several versions of these plans, some offered by states and some by the colleges themselves. Some require prepayment of tuition, as much as all four years in advance, guaranteeing the prevailing rate during the student's freshman year. Others require no prepayment, but still guarantee tuition will not be increased after the freshman year. Some require no prepayment, but want a substantial deposit maintained during the college years. Another type of plan guarantees tuition for as many years as parents can pay in advance, one, two, three, or four. Some colleges and some state agencies will help finance loans for paying all or a portion of the student's tuition in advance, usually at favorable rates.

Some private colleges, and at least three state college systems (Michigan, Florida and Wyoming), allow you to pay for tuition from 1 to 18 years in advance at the current rate. Parents make either a lump-sum investment or periodic payments. The catch for the school (public or private) is taking the risk of actually guaranteeing tuition and hoping that their investment of the funds will make up the difference in rising costs.

Another alternative, which is more common among states, is allowing families to purchase bonds with tax-free income. Of course, the long range plans of prepaying a student's tuition when he or she is just learning their ABCs, does limit where the child may attend. Some states are considering reciprocal agreements that would broaden the choices. If a child chooses not to attend the school, the principal is returned, but some or possibly all of the interest earned may be retained.

Taking advantage of prepaid tuition plans is worth checking into, especially if tuition fees at the college have risen substantially from year to year in the past. However, parents should also consider whether they would receive a better return on their money than the rate of tuition increase. Remember, whether parents pay one, two, three, or the full four years in advance, the college gets to use the money, not the family.

Finally, there are various installment plans, prepayment discount plans, family plans, tuition-equalization plans, alumni plans, and even plans that allow payment by credit card that are available at many private and public institutions. If a student or his parents qualify, these can provide added relief to the overall costs.

***Series EE U.S. Savings Bonds.*** This is one of the newest and best deals around, having just become effective January 1, 1990. Now, proceeds from these bonds are tax exempt as long as they are used to finance a college education or vocational school. Parents, however, must meet certain income criteria (joint adjusted gross income of no more than $60,000, single parent income no more than $40,000). For families with higher incomes, the benefits decline proportionately and disappear completely for joint incomes above $90,000 and single parents earning over $55,000. Bond purchasers must be over 24 years old. This represents a good, safe option guaranteeing families a rate of at least 6 percent and as high as nearly 8 percent.

For more information on tax-free savings bonds for education, write the Department of the Treasury for "The Savings Bond Question and Answer Book" (Item 444X, $.50) and "U.S. Savings Bonds: Now Tax-Free for Education" (Item 445X, $.50). Send to: Consumer Information Center, Dept. 32, Pueblo, CO 81009.

***Life Insurance.*** Using life insurance has several advantages for building funds for college and is one of the most popular methods utilized today for financing a college education:

- The cash value of the policy is not considered an asset when applying for financial aid.
- If a parent dies before the child is old enough for college, the money from the death benefit will help pay for his/her education.
- The cash value increases on a tax-deferred basis while the policy is in force, including dividends.
- The parents can borrow against the cash value of the policy when the child enters college, usually at favorable interest rates, or the accumulated dividends can be surrendered.

Examples of life insurance policies that have differing benefits, savings, and tax advantages include: whole life, variable life, universal life, endowment policies, and single-premium life. Two things, however, are very important to remember: (1) make sure any of these policies is recommended through a qualified financial planner or competent financial adviser, and (2) carefully consider all the benefits and advantages for the family, and not just the one for financing a child's education.

***Home Equity Loans.*** Home equity loans are an easy and flexible way to obtain cash flow on favorable terms, especially if the value of the home has greatly appreciated over the years. The proceeds of such a loan can be used to finance college, and you can deduct the interest on your taxes. However, like life insurance, carefully consider the costs involved (high fees and administrative costs), as well as the interest payments and what it means in the long run to use the family home as collateral for this purpose.

***Zero Coupon Bonds.*** These bonds don't pay semiannual interest as most bonds do, but they can be bought at deep discounts and have a guaranteed full face value when cashed in at a set date. Even though you don't receive the income now, it is compounded semiannually.

Many families use zero coupon bonds because they can time the maturity dates to coincide with their child's college years, since you pick the year you want them to mature in. Parents know how much money these bonds will bring them when those tuition bills come due. These bonds can be municipal bonds, also known as "baccalaureate bonds" (see below), corporate bonds, and U.S. Treasury bonds stripped of their interest coupons. The drawback for most zeros is that, even though you do not receive the interest, you still have to pay the yearly taxes on the accrued interest on the taxable bonds. Nevertheless, at some future date you are receiving a sum that is considerably larger than the purchase price.

"Baccalaureate bonds" are available in over 15 states to buyers who live in the issuing state. They are sold by stockbrokers and, like other zeros, are bought at a deep discount to face value. These are municipal bonds that are exempt from federal, state, and local tax liabilities. Their advantage is that, unlike other municipal bonds, they cannot be redeemed early or "called" by the issuer. However, like other zeros, their market value fluctuates with interest rates and can lose your money if sold early. Another disadvantage is that they tend to sell out quickly and aren't always available, since they actually can be used for any purpose in addition to college savings.

***Annuities, Certificates of Deposit, Stock Market Mutual Funds, Treasury Bonds and Municipal Bonds.*** Investing in these through mutual funds, individual purchases, or special bank savings plans is another innovate way to make long-range plans for paying for college. A couple of tips on investing in tax-free bonds, the stock market, and CDs: Buy tax-free bonds for children under age 14, since the investment income of children under this age is taxed at the parents' tax rates. If parents are in a high tax bracket, using these bonds eliminates this high tax. Also avoid buying tax-free bonds that mature when your child reaches college age. After 14, the income is taxed at your child's tax rate and if they have no other income, they will not be in a high enough tax bracket to justify owning the bonds.

When buying CDs, use several different banks and savings and loans if your CDs are longer than 10 years. By spreading out your CD purchases, you increase the odds that the institutions you've invested in will be in existence 10 years from now when you need the money. Also spread out the maturity dates of your CDs. This will help balance your eventual yields, since over time interest rates have a tendency to move up and down.

With stock market funds, try dollar-cost averaging, which eliminates the hazards of market timing by contributing equal amounts over a long period of time. You buy fewer shares when prices are up and more when prices are down, lowering your average share cost and saving trying to guess when are the best times to buy and sell. Another good idea is to choose a mix of stock funds that will perform well under differing circumstances and changing economic conditions. Again, a trusted and competent, licensed professional investment/financial advisor should be consulted to insure your are choosing the most practical, sensible investments for college planning.

***Giving Gifts and Setting Up Trusts.*** The main purpose of these is to save tax dollars by shifting income from the parents to the children. One way is to give a gift. An individual can make a $10,000 tax-free gift to an individual (or a married couple can give up to $20,000) per year without paying federal gift tax. This is a very good idea for grandparents, since it reduces their estate and eventually will help reduce estate taxes that may be due.

If parents are worried about giving sizable amounts of money to their children, they can still make the gift and keep control of the assets by setting up a custodial account under the Uniform Gifts to Minors Act (UGMA). The custodian is responsible for managing the money in the fund until the minor reaches the age of majority, which can be 18, 19, 20, or 2l. Annual income over $1,000 in a UGMA account is taxed at the parents' rate until the child reaches 14. After that, the income is taxed at the child's rate.

Another possible solution is to set up a Minor's Trust, especially when a substantial amount of money is involved. In this case, the first $5,000 earned by the trust is taxed at a flat 15 percent, the rest at 28 percent. Also, the trustee has control of the funds until the child reaches 21, well into the college paying years. At that time the child has 30 to 60 days to demand the assets from the trust. If he fails to do so, the trust continues until the time designated in the trust agreement.

***Putting the Children on the Payroll.*** This is another income-shifting possibility. By paying a child through the family business, up to $3,000 can be earned tax-free by the child, and the business can take a tax deduction on the earnings paid. Also, up to the age of 18, Social Security taxes do not have to be paid. Keep in mind, however, that the pay must represent a fair value of the work performed by the child, with the child's age and capabilities being considered.

***Buying Property Near a Campus.*** Whether the parent or student buys the property (house, condo), the student can offset his college costs by living on the property. If the property appreciates in value and is sold after graduation, the profits can be considered long-term capital gains. If part of the property is rented out to other students (subleting bedrooms in a home), the rental income can help offset mortgage payments.

If the property is run as a business (the student can also be paid as a residential property manager), then the assets used to buy the property can be shifted to the business category, thus reducing the personal assets of the parents (important for that financial aid application). The parents can also take annual reductions for mortgage interest, operating costs and depreciation on the property.

***Borrowing Against Pension Plans, Keoughs, and IRA's.*** Doing this may involve paying some penalties, but it serves to shift the money from the parents' income account and puts it into an asset account where it receives a lower evaluation when being considered for a financial aid package.

# APPENDIX I

# A GLOSSARY OF FINANCIAL AID "BUZZ WORDS"

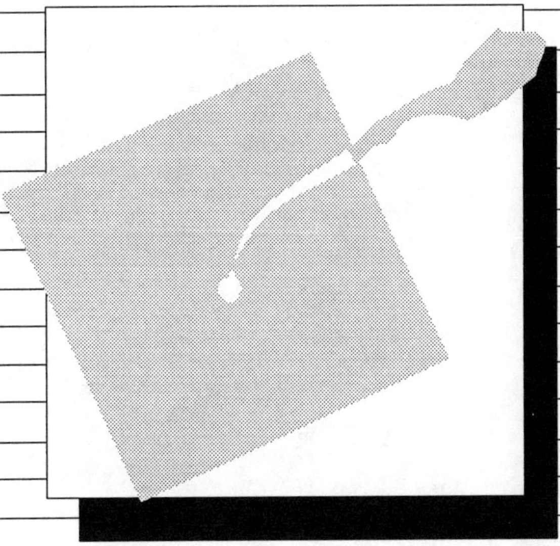

# A GLOSSARY OF FINANCIAL AID "BUZZ WORDS"

At first glance, this may seem somewhat basic, but in order to successfully work through the tangle of the financial aid process, from beginning to end, it is necessary to know the terms and their specific meanings. In other words, you've got to "speak their language" in order to play ball with them. In this case, when it comes to the extremely important matter of financing a college education, the name of the game is "hard ball." The following are terms you will need to know when dealing in the complex world of financial aid applications and formulas, officers and administrators, choices and types of aid, and financial aid awards.

**Accelerated Program.** A concentrated college program of study completed in less time than is normally required.

**Accreditation.** The process that ensures the school's programs maintain at least the minimum standards of quality. Students who attend a nonaccredited program or school will not be eligible for federal or state aid.

**Acknowledgement Report.** The form parents receive after filing their financial aid form, which shows the estimated family contribution, and summarizes the data previously reported in case any changes are necessary.

**ACT Assessment.** The American College Testing Program admissions test covering English usage, mathematics usage, social studies, reading, and natural sciences.

**Admissions Testing Program (ATP).** College Board program that includes the SAT, Achievement Tests, Advance Placement tests, and reports of test results.

**Advanced Placement.** Credit for college-level high school courses, allowing a student to take advanced-level courses in a certain subject. Usually granted on test results.

**American College Testing Program (ACT).** This organization conducts standardized testing and financial aid needs analysis.

**Assets.** Anything that is owned. Property, cash, money in savings accounts, personal valuables. Used in determining student's financial need.

**Bachelor's Degree.** The degree given for completion of undergraduate college/university programs. A complete program usually takes four years.

**Campus-Based Programs.** These are federal financial aid programs that are administered through the financial aid office of a college.

**Class Rank.** A student's approximate standing in the graduating high school class. Based on grade point average (GPA) in terms of either percentiles or rank order.

**College Board.** A membership organization made up of representatives from college admissions and financial aid offices and secondary school guidance counselors.

**College Scholarship Service (CSS).** A service of the College Board that computes information on the Financial Aid Form and estimates the student and family contribution for financial aid analysis.

**College Work/Study (CWS).** A federally supported program that provides 80 percent of the funds for colleges to offer jobs on and off campus to students with demonstrated financial need.

**Comprehensive Financial Aid Report (CFAR).** The American College Testing Program's statement of the expected family contribution. Based on the Family Financial Statement.

**Consumer Price Index.** A measure of inflation or deflation at the consumer level. The rise and fall of the costs of many consumer products/services are often compared to the CPI.

**Cooperative Education Plan (CO-OP).** A program that enables students to combine work and study, structured as either a work and study schedule within the same term, or a work term alternating with a study term. Often prolongs time for completion of a degree.

**Cost of Education.** This is the total amount it will cost a student to attend a particular school. Includes tuition, fees, books, housing, food, transportation, and any miscellaneous or special expenses. An important consideration when determining a financial aid program.

**Credit by Examination.** Academic credit is given a student who has shown a knowledge or proficiency in a given subject. Credit is applied toward student's degree and/or acceptance through an early admission program.

**Dean/Director of Admissions.** The person in charge of the admissions office at a college.

**Deferred Entrance.** This plan allows students to defer their college entrance for one to three years and guarantees enrollment at the time they choose.

**Dependent Student.** A student who is dependent on one or both parents for financial support. A student is classified as dependent or independent (self-supporting) with regard to financial aid purposes.

**Early Action.** Allows students to learn of the decision on their application prior to the standard April notification date.

**Early Admission.** A program where a high school graduate is accepted to begin college work before graduation. Generally early admission standards are higher than for regular admission.

**Early Decision.** Plans that are offered for applicants who are sure of the college they want to attend and are likely to be accepted by that college. The student is generally notified of the school's decision earlier than usual—by December 15 of the senior year. Accepting an early decision usually requires the student to withdraw any other college applications and agree to graduate from the college that has accepted them.

**Early Notification.** These programs are similar to the early action option. Under this plan applicants must file papers by December 1 in order to receive an admission decision by February 1. If admitted, applicants are not obligated to attend the college that admits them.

**Enrollment Deposit.** Many colleges require a nonrefundable deposit by applicants to reserve space in their incoming class.

**Family Contribution.** An amount calculated according to a standard need analysis formula that represents how much a family will be expected to pay toward a child's college education. The figure includes parental contribution and the student's assets and earnings during college.

**Family Financial Statement (FFS).** The form for information on a family's assets, income and liabilities that is used for evaluating student need (American College Testing Program).

**Financial Aid Form (FAF).** Parents or independent students use this form to list all income, and net assets for the College Scholarship Service in their estimate of the expected family contribution.

**Financial Aid Office.** The office at a school of higher education that is responsible for evaluating students' eligibility for aid and awarding the available funds.

**Financial Aid Package.** This is the total amount of financial aid a student receives. May include public and/or private loans, grants, scholarships, a work/study program.

**Financial Award Letter.** Notification from a financial aid officer or college that tells how much aid is being offered to student. The letter also explains how financial need was determined.

**Financial Need.** The amount left over when the expected family contribution has been subtracted from the cost of education. Generally, students are eligible for financial aid that will cover the amount of financial need.

**Grade Point Average.** A system of scoring a student's academic achievement used by high schools, colleges, and universities. Usually computed on a scale using the following point to grade assignments: A=4, B=3, C=2, D=1, E and F=0.

**Grants.** Awards made for educational purposes which do not have to be paid back. Usually given on the basis of need.

**Guaranteed Student Loan (GSL).** Now referred to as Stafford Loans. Loans available to students through local lenders and guaranteed by the federal government against default.

**Half-Time Study.** Refers to enrollment status (academics) in a college or university. Half-time study is used as an eligibility requirement for federal financial aid awards and loans. Measurement of half-time differs from campus to campus.

**Independent Student.** A student who meets the federal criteria for being financially self-supporting. Used in determining student's financial need.

**Interest.** The fee charged by lenders for lending or borrowing money.

**Loan.** Borrowed money that must be repaid. Long term loans with low interest are provided by both colleges and outside sources such as the federal government or private institutions. Short-term loans usually come from college funds.

**National Merit Scholarships.** A national awards program for students selected on the basis of PSAT/NMSQT scores and other criteria.

**Need Analysis.** The method used to determine how much a family will be expected to contribute to the cost of education for college. Usually based on the assumption that the student and his/her parents will have the major responsibility for college costs according to their ability. Generally calculated by a need analysis service.

**Open Admission.** A policy used by many institutions (especially public schools) that allows all applicants to be accepted without regard to the traditional criteria for acceptance, such as class rank, grades, test scores.

**Parental Contribution.** The amount a student's parents are expected to contribute toward college expenses.

**Pell Grants.** This is the largest federally funded aid program. This is a college-based program, meaning the funds are actually disbursed by the colleges to all applying students who qualify for aid. An outright gift program, with no strings attached.

**Preliminary Scholastic Aptitude Test/National Merit Scholarship Qualifying Test (PSAT/NMSQT).** A short version of the SAT that gives a student a preview sample of what the SAT will be like and also serves as the qualifying basis for the National Merit Scholarship Corporation's scholarship competition.

**Remaining Need.** The difference between the total amount of a student's cost of education and the amount of financial aid plus the family contribution. Cost of attendance = family contribution + aid + remaining need. The remaining need determines whether a student qualifies for a Stafford (low-interest, federal) Loan.

**Reserve Officers' Training Corps (ROTC).** A training and scholarship program offered by the Army, Navy, Marines, and Air Force offered at more than 600 college campuses. A service obligation following graduation is required.

**Rolling Admissions.** A program in which admissions applications are evaluated when received, and applicants are immediately notified of the decision.

**Scholarship.** A financial award, paid directly to a student or a college, that does not have to be paid back. Usually based on talent or scholastic excellence in a particular area. Can be based on need or non-need. Need-based scholarships are usually awarded in combination with a financial aid package. Non-need awards are given in recognition of special talents or qualities.

**Scholastic Aptitude Test (SAT).** The standardized test from the College Board Admissions Testing Program. Includes a verbal section, math section, and a test of written English.

**Standardized Admissions Test.** The term referring to tests such as the ACT and SAT used by nearly all college admissions offices and many sponsors of student aid programs for rating a student's academic aptitude for admissions consideration and awarding financial aid.

**Student Aid Report (SAR).** The report sent to a student applying for federal student aid containing information to guide financial aid officers in determining amount of a Pell Grant.

**Student's Contribution.** The amount a student is expected to pay toward college costs calculated from expected income, assets, and benefits. The student contribution plus the parental contribution makes up the total family contribution portion of the need analysis formula.

# APPENDIX
# II
# STATE BY STATE GUARANTEED STUDENT LOAN PROGRAM SOURCES

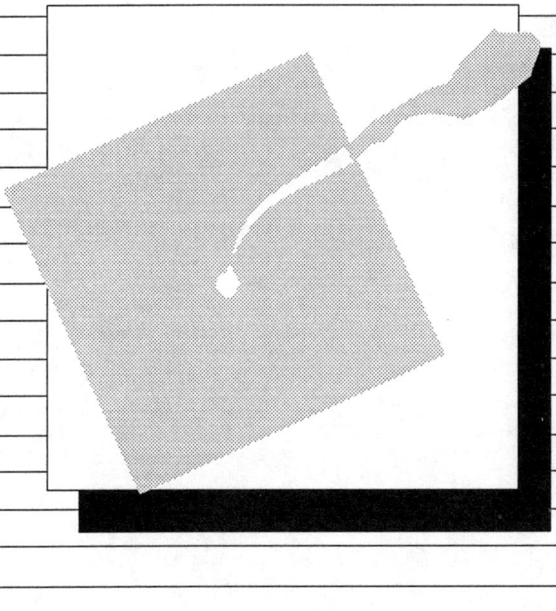

# STATE BY STATE GUARANTEED STUDENT LOAN PROGRAM SOURCES

**ALABAMA**
Alabama Commission on
Higher Education
One Court Square, Suite 221
Montgomery, AL 36197
(205) 269-2700

**ALASKA**
Alaska Commission on
Postsecondary Education
400 Willoughby Ave.,
P.O. Box FP
Juneau, AK 99811
(907) 465-2962

**ARIZONA**
Arizona Educational
Loan Program
1400 E. Southern Ave.
Tempe, AZ 85282
(602) 831-9988

**ARKANSAS**
Arkansas Department of
Higher Education
1220 West Third Street
Little Rock, AR 72201
(501) 371-1441

**CALIFORNIA**
California Student Aid
Commission
1410 Fifth Street
Sacramento,CA 95814
(916) 445-0880

**COLORADO**
Colorado Commission
on Higher Education
1300 Broadway, 2nd Floor
Denver, CO 80203
(303) 866-2723

**CONNECTICUT**
Connecticut Department
of Higher Education
61 Woodland Street
Hartford, CT 06105
(203) 566-2618

**DELAWARE**
Delaware Postsecondary
Education Commission
820 North French St., 4th Floor
Wilmington, DE 19801
(302) 571-3240

**DISTRICT OF COLUMBIA**
H.E.L.P., D.C.
1225 Street, N.W., Suite 500
Washington, DC 20005
(202) 289-4500

**FLORIDA**
Office of Student Financial Assistance
Department of Education
Knott Building
Tallahassee, FL 32399
(904) 488-4095

**GEORGIA**
Georgia Student Finance Authority
2082 East Exchange Place, #200
Tucker, GA 30084
(404) 493-5444

**HAWAII**
Hawaii Education Loan Program
P.O. Box 22187
Honolulu, HI 96823-2187
(808) 536-3731

**IDAHO**
Student Loan Fund of Idaho
P.O. Box 730
Fruitland, ID 83619
(800) 528-9447

**ILLINOIS**
Illinois State Scholarship Commission
106 Wilmot Road
Deerfield, IL 60015
(708) 948-8550

**INDIANA**
State Student Assistance Commission
964 North Pennsylvania Ave.
1st Floor
Indianapolis, IN 46204
(317) 232-2350

**IOWA**
Iowa College Aid Commission
201 Jewett Building
North and Grand
Des Moines, IA 50309
(515) 281-3501

**KANSAS**
Kansas Board of Regents
Capitol Tower, Suite 609
400 Southwest Eighth St.
Topeka, KS 66603
(913) 296-3517

**KENTUCKY**
Kentucky Higher Education Authority
1050 U.S. 127 South
Frankfort, KY 40601
(502) 564-7990

**LOUISIANA**
Governor's Special Commission on Education Services
P.O. Box 91202
Baton Rouge, LA 70804
(504) 922-1038

**MAINE**
Department of Educational and Cultural Services
Higher Education Services
State House Station 119
Augusta, ME 04333
(207) 289-2183

**MARYLAND**
Maryland Higher
Education Loan Corporation
2100 Guilford Avenue
Baltimore, MD 21218
(301) 333-6420

**MASSACHUSETTS**
Higher Education
Assistance Corp.
330 Stuart St.
Boston, MA 02116
(617) 727-9420

**MICHIGAN**
Michigan Department
of Education
Guaranteed Student
Loan Program
Ottawa Bldg. South, 1st Floor
P.O. Box 30008
Lansing, MI 48909
(517) 373-3394

**MINNESOTA**
Minnesota Higher Education
Coordinating Board
Suite 400, Capitol Square Bldg.
550 Cedar Street
St. Paul, MN 55101
(612) 296-3974

**MISSISSIPPI**
Mississippi Guaranteed
Student Loan Agency
3825 Ridgewood Road
P.O. Box 342
Jackson, MS 39205-0342
(601) 982-6663

**MISSOURI**
Coordinating Board for Higher
Education
P.O. Box 1438
Jefferson City, MO 65102
(314) 751-3940

**MONTANA**
Office of the Commissioner of
Higher Education
Montana University System
35 Last Chance Gulch
Helena, MT 59620
(406) 444-6594

**NEBRASKA**
Nebraska Higher Education
Loan Program (NEBHELP)
1300 O Street
Lincoln, NE 68501
(800) 735-8778

**NEVADA**
Financial Aid Office
Student Financial
Services/076
University of Nevada, Reno
Reno, NV 89557
(702) 784-4666

**NEW HAMPSHIRE**
New Hampshire Postsecondary
Education Commission
2-1/2 Beacon Street
Concord, NH 03301
(603) 271-2555

**NEW JERSEY**
Department of Higher Education
Office of Student Assistance
4 Quakerbridge Plaza, CN 540
Trenton, NJ 08625
(609) 588-3272;
(800) 792-8670

**NEW MEXICO**
New Mexico Education Assistance Foundation
1068 Cerrillos Road
Santa Fe, NM 87503
(505) 827-8300

**NEW YORK**
Higher Education Services Corp.
99 Washington Ave., 14th Floor
Albany, NY 12255
(518) 474-5642

**NORTH CAROLINA**
North Carolina State Education Assistance Authority
Box 2688
Chapel Hill, NC 27515
(919) 549-8614

**NORTH DAKOTA**
Student Financial Assistance Program
State Capitol, 10th Floor
Bismarck, ND 58505
(701) 224-4114

**OHIO**
Student Assistance Office
Ohio Board of Regents
3600 State Office Tower
30 East Broad Street
Columbus, OH 43266
(614) 466-7420

**OKLAHOMA**
Oklahoma State Regents for Higher Education
500 Education Building
State Capitol Complex
Oklahoma City, OK 73105
(405) 521-2444

**OREGON**
Oregon State Scholarship Commission
1445 Willamette Street, #9
Eugene, OR 97401
(503) 686-4166

**PENNSYLVANIA**
Pennsylvania Higher Education Assistance Agency
660 Boas Street, Townhouse
Harrisburg, PA 17102
(717) 257-2800; (800) 692-7435

**RHODE ISLAND**
Rhode Island Higher Education Assistance Authority
560 Jefferson Blvd.
Warwick, RI 02886
(401) 277-2050

**SOUTH CAROLINA**
South Carolina Tuition Grants Commission
411 Keenan Building
P.O. Box 12259
Columbia, SC 29211
(803) 734-1200

**SOUTH DAKOTA**
Department of Education and Cultural Affairs
Office of the Secretary
700 Governors Drive
Pierre, SD 57501
(605) 773-3134

**TENNESSEE**
Tennessee Student
Assistance Corp.
Parkway Towers, Suite 1950
404 James Robertson Parkway
Nashville, TN 37219-5097
(615) 741-1346; (800) 342-1663

**TEXAS**
Texas Higher Education
Coordinating Board
Texas College and
University System
Box 12788, Capitol Station
Austin, TX 78711
(512) 462-6325

**UTAH**
Loan Servicing
Corporation of Utah
P.O. Box 30802
1128 West 2400 South
Salt Lake City, UT 84130-0802
(801) 975-2222

**VERMONT**
Vermont Student
Assistance Corp.
Champlain Mill
P.O. Box 2000
Winooski, VT 05404
(802) 655-9602

**VIRGINIA**
State Council of Higher
Education for Virginia
James Monroe Building
1010 North Fourteenth Street
Richmond, VA 23219
(804) 225-2141

**WASHINGTON**
Higher Education
Coordinating Board
917 Lakeridge Way
Olympia, WA 98504
(206) 753-3571

**WEST VIRGINIA**
West Virginia Board of Regents
Higher Education
Grant Program
P.O. Box 4007
Charleston, WV 25364
(304) 347-1211

**WISCONSIN**
Wisconsin Higher
Educational Aids Board
P.O. Box 7885
Madison, WI 53707
(608) 266-2578

**WYOMING**
Wyoming Community
College Commission
122 W. 25th St.
Herschler Bldg., 2 West, Suite 2610
Cheyenne, WY 82202
(307) 777-7763

**GUAM**
Financial Aid Office
University of Guam
UOG Station
Mangilao, Guam 96923
(617) 734-2921 x3657

**PUERTO RICO**
Council on Higher Education
Box F-UPR Station, Box 23305
San Juan, Puerto Rico 00931
(819) 758-3350

**VIRGIN ISLANDS**
Financial Aid Office
Virgin Islands Board
of Education
P.O. Box 11900
St. Thomas, Virgin Islands 00801
(809) 774-4546

# APPENDIX III
## REFERENCES: FINANCIAL AID SOURCES AND INFORMATION

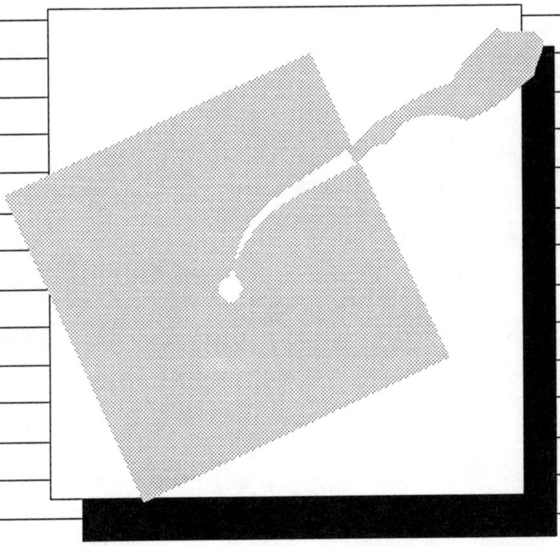

# REFERENCES: FINANCIAL AID SOURCES AND INFORMATION

Note: Check your local library and bookstores for many of the publications listed below, especially the in-depth annual guides and directories for financial aid (which libraries subscribe to yearly). Always make sure you are using the latest edition available in a reference guide or listing.

## GENERAL

***Advanced Placement Program***, College Entrance Exam Board, 888 Seventh Ave., New York, NY 10106.

***Advisory List of National Contests and Activities***, National Association of Secondary School Principals, 1904 Association Drive, Reston, VA 22091.

***American College Testing Program***, Box 168, Iowa City, IA 52240. (For requesting copies of the ACT "Family Financial Statement".)

***Annual Register of Grant Support***, $110, National Register Publishing Co., 3004 Glenview Rd., Wilmette, IL 60091.

***College Cost Planner***, P.O. Box 18623, Washington, D.C. 20077. (Monthly publication of information regarding postsecondary education.)

**College Scholarship Service**, Box 2700, Princeton, NJ 08541 or Box 380, Berkeley, CA 34701. (For requesting copies of the CSS "Financial Aid Form.")

***Corporate Tuition Aid Program: A Directory of College Financial Aid for Employees at America's Largest Corporations***, Conference University Press, Princeton, NJ.

***Directory of Financial Aids for the Disabled and Their Dependents***, Reference Service Press. 10 Twin Dolphin Drive, Suite B-308, Redwood City, CA 94065.

***Don't Miss Out - The Ambitious Student's Guide to Financial Aid***, Ann J. and Robert Leider, Octameron Associates, $5, P.O. Box 33437, Alexandria, VA 22302. (Send for catalog of other Octameron publications.)

***Federal Student Aid Information Center Hotline***, United States Department of Education, Office of Student Financial Assistance. Direct questions to: (800) 333-INFO.

***Financial Aids for Higher Education***, by Oreon Keeslar, $36.80, Wm. C. Brown Company, 2460 Kerper Blvd, Dubuque, IA 52001.

***Foundation Directory***, $85. The Foundation Center, 79 5th Avenue, New York, NY 10003.

***Foundation Grants to Individuals***, $24, by Loren Renz, Foundation Center, 79 5th Avenue, 8th Floor, New York, NY 10003.

***Getting Yours: The Complete Guide to Government Money***, by Matthew Lesko, $8.95, Penguin Books, Order Dept., 299 Murray Hill Parkway, East Rutherford, NJ 07073.

***Grants Register***, by Norman Frankel, $59.95,
St. Martin's Press, New York, NY.

***Higher Education Assistance Foundation***
P.O. Box 6407, St. Paul, MN 55164.

***How and Where to Get Scholarships and Financial Aid for College***, Arco, New York, NY.

***How to Find Out About Financial Aid: A Guide to Over 700 Directories***, $32.50, by Gail Ann Schlacter, Reference Service Press, Suite 9, 1100 Industrial Road, San Carlos, CA 94070.

***Lovejoy's Guide to Financial Aid***, by Robert Leider,
Monarch Books, New York, NY.

***National Merit Scholarship Corporation (NMSC)***, One Rotary Center, 1560 Sherman Avenue, Evanston, IL 6020l.

***"Need A Lift?,"*** $2 The American Legion, Emblem Sales, P.O. Box 1050, Indianapolis, IN 46206.

***The Pell Grant Formula***, Federal Student Financial Aid Program, Box 84, Washington, D.C. 20044.

***Preliminary Scholastic Aptitude Test/National Merit Scholarship Qualifying Test (PSAT/NMSQT)***, P.O.Box 24700, Oakland, CA 94623-1700.

***"Sources of Information on Student Aid,"*** National Education Association, 1201 16th St., N.W., Washington, D.C. 20036.

***Student Aid Annual, Student Aid Bulletins***, $21.95, Chronicle Guidance Publications, Inc., Aurora Street, P.O. Box 1190, Moravia, NY 13118. (Send for catalog of Chronicle publications.)

***The Citizens Scholarship Foundation of America***, Box 112A, RFD #7, Manchester, NH 03107.

***The College Blue Book: Scholarships, Fellowships, Grants and Loans,*** $48, MacMillan Publishing Co, 866 Third Street, New York, NY 10022.

***The College Cost Book***, $10.95, College Board Publications Orders, Box 886, New York, NY 10101.

***The College Financial Aid Emergency Kit***, by Dr. Herm Davis and Joyce Lain Kennedy, $4.50, Sun Features, Box 368-II, Cardiff, CA 92007.

***The College Handbook***, $16.95, College Board Publications Orders, Box 886, New York, NY 10101.

***The College-Level Examination Program (CLEP)***, CLEP, The College Board, 888 Seventh Avenue, New York, NY 10106.

***The College Money Book***, by Gene R. Hawes and David M. Brownstone, Bobbs-Merrill Company, Inc., 630 Third Ave., New York, NY 10017.

***The College Money Handbook***, Peterson's Guide, Princeton, NJ.

***The Scholarship Book***, by Daniel J. Cassidy and Michael J. Alves, Prentice Hall, Englewood Cliffs, NJ 07632.

***"The Student Guide: Five Federal Financial Aid Programs,"*** free, Student Guide, Dept. 511T, Consumer Information Center, Pueblo, CO 81009 or P.O. Box 92831, Los Angeles, CA 90009.

***Undergraduate Programs of Cooperative Education in the United States and Canada***, National Commission for Cooperative Education, 360 Huntington Ave., Boston, MA 02115.

# MILITARY

## *Health Profession Scholarship Programs*

**Air Force**: Health Professions Recruiting, Building 1413, Stop 44, Andrews Air Force Base, MD 20331.

**Army**: Student Programs Management, Department of the Army (SGPE-PDM), 1900 Half Street, N.W., Washington, D.C. 20324.

**Navy and Marines**: Bureau of Medicine and Surgery, (MED-214), Navy Department, Washington, D.C. 20372.

## *Military Academy Programs*

**Air Force**: Director of Cadet Admissions, Air Force Academy, Colorado Springs, CO 80840.

**Army**: Admissions Office, U.S. Military Academy, West Point, NY 10096.

**Navy**: U.S. Naval Academy, Candidate Guidance Office, Annapolis, MD 21402.

**Coast Guard:** Director of Admissions, U.S. Coast Guard Academy, New London, CT 06320.

**Merchant Marine**: Admissions Office, U.S. Merchant Marine Academy, Kings Point, NY 11024.

## ROTC Programs

**Air Force**: Air Force ROTC, Office of Public Affairs, Maxwell AFB, AL 36112.

**Army**: Army ROTC Scholarship Program, Fort Monroe, VA 23651.

**Navy and Marines**: NROTC Scholarship Programs, 4015 Wilson Blvd., Arlington, VA 22203.

## Veterans Administration and Social Security Administration Financial Aid Programs

**Division of Student Services and Veterans Programs,** 400 Maryland Avenue, S.W., Room 400, Washington, D.C., 20202.

**VEA (Veterans Education Assistance Act) Benefits** Program, REACT Center,P.O.Box 1000, Mt.Vernon, NY 10550.

## Other

***How the Military Will Help You Pay for College***, by Don M. Betterton, $6.95, Peterson's Guides, 166 Bunn Dr., P.O.Box 2123, Princeton, NJ. Gives extensive information about scholarship and financial aid opportunities for students considering all areas of military service in connection with scholarship and tuition- paying programs.

# SPECIFIC POPULATION GROUPS

***American Association of University Women***, Educational Foundation Programs Office, 2401 Virginia Avenue, N.W., Washington, D.C. 20037.

***"Athletic Scholarships for Women,"*** $2, Women's Sports Foundation, 342 Madison Ave., Suite 728, New York, NY 10173.

***Bureau of Indian Affairs Higher Education Grants and Scholarships***, Bureau of Indian Affairs, Code 522-Room 3512, 19th and C Streets, Washington, D.C. 20240.

***Business and Professional Women's Foundation***, 2021 Massachusetts Avenue, N.W., Washington, D.C. 20036.

***Directory of Financial Aids for Minorities***, $45, Reference Service Press, 1100 Industrial Road, Suite 9, San Carlos, CA 94070. (Contains references and cross-references to scholarships, fellowships, grants, loans, awards and internships for ethnic minorities.)

***Directory of Financial Aids for Women***, $42.50, Reference Service Press, 1100 Industrial Road, Suite 9, San Carlos, CA 94070.

***Directory of Special Programs for Minority Group Members: Career Information Services, Employment Skills Banks, Financial Aid Sources***, $22.50, Garrett Park Press, P.O. Box 190, Garrett Park, MD 20896. Also published by Garrett:

> ***Financial Aid for Minorities in Business and Law*** ($4).
>
> ***Financial Aid for Minorities in Education*** ($4).
>
> ***Financial Aid for Minorities in Engineering and Science*** ($4).
>
> ***Financial Aid for Minorities in Health Fields*** ($4).
>
> ***Financial Aid for Minorities in Journalism and Mass Communication*** ($4).
>
> ***Financial Aid for Minorities: Awards Open to Students with Any Major*** ($4).
>
> ***Directory of Special Opportunities for Women*** ($18).

***"Financial Aid to Education,"*** Knights of Columbus, 1 Columbus Plaza, New Haven, CT 06507. (Contains information about loans and scholarships for children of members of the Knights of Columbus.)

***Grants Register***, by Norman Frankel, $59.95, St. Martin's Press, New York, NY.

***Higher Education Opportunities for Minorities and Women***, $5.50, Superintendent of Documents, U.S. Government Printing Office, Washington, D.C. 20402-9325.

***Hispanic Financial Resource Handbook***, $7, The Office of Hispanic Student Programs, Ohio State University, 347 Ohio Union, 1739 N. High Street, Columbus, OH 43210.

# APPENDIX IV

## SAMPLE STUDENT AID FORMS AND APPLICATIONS

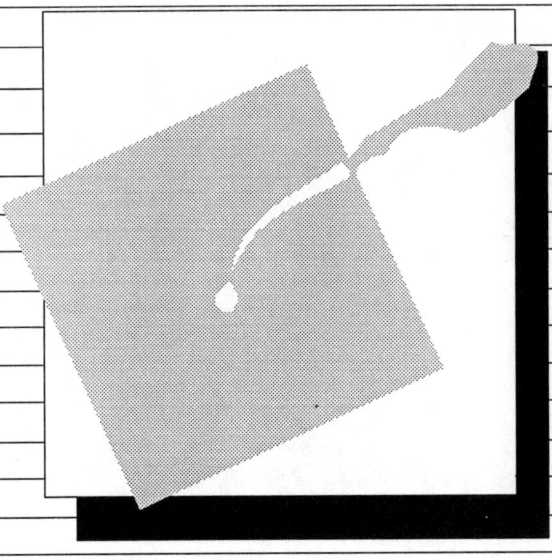

# STUDENT AID APPLICATION FOR CALIFORNIA (SAAC)

**COLLEGE SCHOLARSHIP SERVICE (CSS)**

**CALIFORNIA STUDENT AID COMMISSION**

**THE COLLEGE BOARD**

**SAAC** **Student Aid Application for California** — School Year 1990-91

Warning: If you use this form to establish eligibility for federal student aid and you purposely give false or misleading information, you may be subject to a $10,000 fine, a prison sentence, or both.

Do not write in this space.

Use only a No. 2 (soft lead) pencil. Don't write outside of the boxes or answer spaces. "You" and "your" on this form always means the student who wants aid.

CA O

## Section A — Student's Identification Information

1. Your name ______ Last ______ First ______ M.I.
2. Your permanent mailing address (Mail will be sent to this address. See page 5 for state/country abbreviation.) ______ Number, street, and apartment number ______ City ______ State ______ Zip Code
3. Your title (optional) 1 ☐ Mr. 2 ☐ Miss, Ms., or Mrs.
4. Your state of legal residence ☐
5. Your social security number ___-__-____
6. Your date of birth ☐ Month ☐ Day ☐ Year
7. Are you a U.S. citizen? (Mark only one box.)
   1 ☐ Yes, I am a U.S. citizen.
   2 ☐ No, but I am an eligible noncitizen. (See the instructions on page 5.) A ______
   3 ☐ No, neither of the above. (See the instructions on page 5.)
8. As of today, are you married? (Mark only one box.)
   1 ☐ I am not married. (I am single, divorced, or widowed.)
   2 ☐ I am married.
   3 ☐ I am separated from my spouse.
9. What year will you be in college in 1990-91? (Mark only one box.)
   1 ☐ 1st (never previously attended college)
   2 ☐ 1st (previously attended college)
   3 ☐ 2nd
   4 ☐ 3rd
   5 ☐ 4th
   6 ☐ 5th or more undergraduate
   7 ☐ first year graduat[e] professional (beyo[nd] a bachelor's degr[ee])
   8 ☐ continuing gradua[te] or professional
10. Will you have your first bachelor's degree before July 1, 1990? Yes ☐1 No ☐

## Section B — Student Status

11. a. Were you born **before** January 1, 1967? Yes ☐1 No ☐2
    b. Are you a veteran of the U.S. Armed Forces? Yes ☐1 No ☐2
    c. Are you a ward of the court or are both your parents dead? Yes ☐1 No ☐2
    d. Do you have legal dependents (other than a spouse) that fit the definition in the instructions on page 5? Yes ☐1 No ☐2

- If you answered "Yes" to any part of question **11**, go to Section C and fill in th[e] **GRAY** and the **WHITE** areas on the rest of the form. Some colleges may also a[sk] you to complete the **BLUE** areas. (Skip questions **12** through **15**.)
- If you answered "No" to every part of question **11** and you are:
  —unmarried now (single, divorced, separated, or widowed) **and** will be an undergra[d]uate student in 1990-91, answer question **12**. (Skip question **15**.)
  —married now or will be a graduate/professional student in 1990-91, answer questi[on] **15**. Skip questions **12** through **14d**.)

### Unmarried Undergraduate Students Only

12. Did your parents claim you as an income tax exemption ...in 1988? Yes ☐1 No ☐2 ...in 1989? Yes ☐1 No ☐2

- If you answered "Yes" to **either** year in question **12**, go to Section C and fill in th[e] **BLUE** and the **WHITE** areas on the rest of the form. (Skip questions **13** through **15**.)
- If you answered "No" to **both** years in question **12**, answer question **13** below.

13. Beginning with the 1987-88 school year, when did you **first** receive federal student financial aid? (Mark only one box. See instructions on pages 5-6.)
    1 ☐ During the 1987-88 school year (Answer **14a** only. Skip questions **14b**, **14c**, and **14d**.)
    2 ☐ During the 1988-89 school year (Answer **14b** only. Skip questions **14a**, **14c**, and **14d**.)
    3 ☐ During the 1989-90 school year (Answer **14c** only. Skip questions **14a**, **14b**, and **14d**.)
    4 ☐ In neither 1, nor 2, nor 3. (Answer **14d** only. Skip questions **14a**, **14b**, and **14c**.)

14. a. Did you have total resources of $4,000 or more, not including parents' support ...in 1985? Yes ☐1 No ☐2 ...in 1986? Yes ☐1 No ☐
14. b. Did you have total resources of $4,000 or more, not including parents' support ...in 1986? Yes ☐1 No ☐2 ...in 1987? Yes ☐1 No ☐
14. c. Did you have total resources of $4,000 or more, not including parents' support ...in 1987? Yes ☐1 No ☐2 ...in 1988? Yes ☐1 No ☐
14. d. Did you have total resources of $4,000 or more, not including parents' support ...in 1988? Yes ☐1 No ☐2 ...in 1989? Yes ☐1 No ☐

After you answer **14a**, **14b**, **14c**, or **14d**, follow the instructions at the right.

- If you answered "No" to **either** year in question **14a**, **14b**, **14c**, or **14d**, go to Section C and fill in the **BLUE** a[nd] the **WHITE** areas on the rest of the form.
- If you answered "Yes" to **both** years in question **14a**, **14b**, **14c**, or **14d**, go to Section C and fill in the **GRAY** a[nd] the **WHITE** areas on the rest of the form. Some colleges may also ask you to complete the **BLUE** areas.

### Married Students or Graduate/Professional Students Only

15. Will your parents claim you as an income tax exemption in 1990? Yes ☐1 No ☐2

- If you answered "Yes" to question **15**, go to Section C and fill in the **BLUE** and the **WHITE** areas on the rest of the form.
- If you answered "No" to question **15**, go to Section C and fill in the **GRAY** and the **WHITE** areas on the rest of the form. Some colleges may also ask you to complete the **BLUE** areas.

## Section C — Household Information

### Parents

16. What is your parents' current marital status? (Mark only one box.) 1 ☐ single 2 ☐ married 3 ☐ separated 4 ☐ divorced 5 ☐ widowed
17. What is your parents' state of legal residence? ☐
18. Number of family members in 1990-91 ☐
    Write in the total number of people your parents will support in 1990-91. **Always include yourself (the student) and your parents.** Include your parents' other children and other people only if they meet the definition in the instructions on page 6.
19. Number of college students in 1990-91 ☐
    Of the number in **18**, write in the number of family members who will be in college at least half-time. Include yourself — the student who is applying for aid.

### Student (and Spouse)

20. **Number of family members in 1990-91** ☐
    **Write in the total number of people that you will support in 1990-91. Include yourself and your spouse. Include your children and other people only if they meet the definition in the instructions on page 6.**
21. **Number of college students in 1990-91** ☐
    **Of the number in 20, write in the number of family members who will be in college at least half-time. Include yourself.**

**Section D — 1989 Income, Earnings, and Benefits** (You must see the instructions for income and taxes that you should exclude from questions **24** through **28.**)

Everyone must fill out the Student (and Spouse) column below.

| | | Parents | Student (and Spouse) |
|---|---|---|---|
| **22.** The following 1989 U.S. income tax return figures are (Mark only one box.) | from a completed IRS Form 1040EZ or 1040A. (Go to **23.**) | 22. 1 ☐ | 22. 1 ☐ |
| | from a completed IRS Form 1040. (Go to **23.**) | 2 ☐ | 2 ☐ |
| | estimated. Will file IRS Form 1040EZ or 1040A. (Go to **23.**) | 3 ☐ | 3 ☐ |
| | estimated. Will file IRS Form 1040. (Go to **23.**) | 4 ☐ | 4 ☐ |
| | a tax return will not be filed. (Skip to **26.**) | 5 ☐ | 5 ☐ |
| Tax Filers Only: **23.** 1989 total number of exemptions (IRS Form 1040 — line 6e, 1040A — line 6e, or 1040EZ — see instructions on pages 6 and 7) | | 23. | 23. |
| **24.** 1989 income from IRS Form 1040 — line 31, 1040A — line 13, or 1040EZ — line 3 (See instructions.) | | 24. $ .00 | 24. $ .00 |
| **25.** 1989 U.S. income tax paid (IRS Form 1040 — line 47, 1040A — line 22, or 1040EZ — line 7) | | 25. $ .00 | 25. $ .00 |
| **26.** 1989 income earned from work by | | **Father** 26. $ .00 | **Student** 26. $ .00 |
| **27.** 1989 income earned from work by | | **Mother** 27. $ .00 | **Spouse** 27. $ .00 |
| **28.** 1989 untaxed income and benefits (yearly totals only) | | | |
| **a.** Social security benefits | | 28a. $ .00 | 28a. $ .00 |
| **b.** Aid to Families with Dependent Children (AFDC or ADC) | | b. $ .00 | b. $ .00 |
| **c.** Child support received for all children | | c. $ .00 | c. $ .00 |
| **d.** Other untaxed 1989 income and benefits from Worksheet II on page 11 of the instructions | | d. $ .00 | d. $ .00 |

**Section E — Federal Student Aid Releases and Certification**

**29.** What college(s) do you plan to go to in 1990-91?

| Name | City and State | CSS Code No. |
|---|---|---|
| | | |
| | | |

**30. a.** Do you give CSS permission to send information from this form to the U.S. Department of Education? (Mark "Yes" if you want to be considered for a Pell Grant and other federal student financial aid. If you answer "No," skip **30b** and **31.**) Yes ☐1 No ☐2

**30. b.** Do you give the U.S. Department of Education permission to send information from this form to:

— the financial aid agency in your state? Yes ☐1 No ☐2

— the college(s) you named in **29** (or its representative)? Yes ☐1 No ☐2

**Note:** By marking "Yes" you are not applying for state and institutional aid in most states. Most agencies and colleges also require that a CSS report be sent to them. See instructions.

**31.** Mark this box if you give Selective Service permission to register you. (See instructions.) ☐

**32. Certification:** All of the information on this form and the Supplemental Information, if completed, is true and complete to the best of my knowledge. If asked by an authorized official, I agree to give proof of the information that I have given on this form and the Supplemental Information, if completed. I realize that this proof may include a copy of my U.S., state, or local income tax return. I also realize that if I don't give proof when asked, the student may be denied aid.

**Everyone giving information on this form must sign below.**

1 ____________ Student's signature

2 ____________ Student's spouse's signature

3 ____________ Father's signature

4 ____________ Mother's signature

**Date this form was completed:** Month Day Year 1 ☐ 1990 2 ☐ 1991

Write in the month and day. Mark the year completed.

**IMPORTANT: You must read the instructions on page 8 to see if you need to fill out Sections F through I.**

**SUPPLEMENTAL INFORMATION**

**Section F — 1989 Expenses**

| | Parents | Student (and Spouse) |
|---|---|---|
| **33.** 1989 medical and dental expenses not paid by insurance | 33. $ .00 | 33. $ .00 |
| **34.** 1989 elementary, junior high, and high school tuition for dependent children **a.** Amount paid (Don't include tuition paid for the applicant.) | 34a. $ .00 | 34a. $ .00 |
| **b.** For how many dependent children? (Don't include the applicant.) | b. | b. |

**Section G — Asset Information**

**If you are completing this section, you must fill out the Student (and Spouse) columns below.**

**Parents**

**35.** Is either of your parents a displaced homemaker? (See instructions on page 8.) 35. Yes ☐1 No ☐2

**36.** Write in the age of your older parent. 36.

**Student (and Spouse)**

**35.** Are you or is your spouse a displaced homemaker? Yes ☐1 No ☐2 (See instructions on page 9.)

**36.** XXXXXXXXXXXXXXXX

| | Parents: What is it worth today? | Parents: What is owed on it? | Student (and Spouse): What is it worth today? | Student (and Spouse): What is owed on it? |
|---|---|---|---|---|
| **37.** Cash, savings, and checking accounts | 37. $ .00 | XXXXXXXXXXXXXXX | 37. $ .00 | XXXXXXXXXXXXXXX |
| **38.** Home (Renters write in "0.") | 38. $ .00 | $ .00 | 38. $ .00 | $ .00 |
| **39.** Other real estate and investments | 39. $ .00 | $ .00 | 39. $ .00 | $ .00 |
| **40.** Business and farm | 40. $ .00 | $ .00 | 40. $ .00 | $ .00 |
| **41.** Does any part of **40** include a farm? | 41. Yes ☐1 No ☐2 | | 41. Yes ☐1 No ☐2 | |

**Section H — Student's Veterans Educational Benefits** (Expected Amount July 1, 1990 – June 30, 1991) (If you are completing this section, you must answer question **42.** If you are filling out the gray and white areas, you must also answer question **43.**)

**42.** Your veterans "old" GI Bill & Dependents Educational Assistance Benefits

**a.** Amount per month $ .00 **b.** Number of months

**43.** Your VA Contributory Benefits (VEAP)

**a.** Amount per month $ .00 **b.** Number of months

Print your name: Last |_|_|_|_|_|_|_|_|_|_|_|_|_|_|_|_|_|_|_| First |_|_|_|_|_|_|_|_|_|_|_|

**Section I — Expected 1990 Taxable & Nontaxable Income & Benefits**
(You must see the instructions for income and taxes that you should exclude from questions **45** through **49**.)

**If you are completing this section, you must fill out the Student (and Spouse) column below.**

| | | Parents | | Student (and Spouse) |
|---|---|---|---|---|
| **44.** Is either parent **certified** as a dislocated worker by the appropriate agency? (See instructions on page 9.) | | **44.** Yes ☐1 No ☐2 | Are you or is your spouse **certified** as a dislocated worker by the appropriate agency? (See instructions on page 9.) | **44.** Yes ☐1 No ☐2 |
| **45.** 1990 U.S. income tax to be paid | | **45.** $ .00 | | **45.** $ .00 |
| **46.** 1990 income earned from work by | **Father** | **46.** $ .00 | **Student** | **46.** $ .00 |
| **47.** 1990 income earned from work by | **Mother** | **47.** $ .00 | **Spouse** | **47.** $ .00 |
| **48.** 1990 other taxable income | | **48.** $ .00 | | **48.** $ .00 |
| **49.** 1990 nontaxable income and benefits (See instructions.) | | **49.** $ .00 | | **49.** $ .00 |

**Section J — Student's Other Information**

**50.** Your home telephone |_|_|_|-|_|_|_|-|_|_|_|_|
Area Code Number

**51.** Give your high school 6-digit code number.
(To be completed only by high school seniors.) |_|_|_|_|_|_|

**52. a.** List all colleges or schools that you have attended since high school. Always list first the college or school most recently attended.

| Name, city, and state of college | Period of attendance From (mo./yr.) | To (mo./yr.) | CSS Code Number |
|---|---|---|---|
| | | | |
| | | | |
| | | | |
| | | | |

**b.** If you have attended more than four colleges or schools, mark here. Give names and CSS code numbers in Section P. ☐

**53. a.** Your current degree/certificate objective (Mark only one box.)

1☐ Certificate
2☐ A.A./Transfer
3☐ B.A./B.S.
4☐ Teaching Credential
5☐ Graduate/Professional
6☐ Other (Specify: ______________ )

**b.** Date you expect to complete your current degree/certificate Month |_|_| Year |_|_|

**54.** During the 1990-91 school year, you want financial aid from |_|_| |_|_| through |_|_| |_|_|
Month Year Month Year

**55.** Mark your preference for work or loan assistance.
1☐ Part-time job only
2☐ Part-time job and loan
3☐ Loan only
4☐ No preference

**Section K — Student's Other Income**
(See instructions for the kinds of income to exclude.)

| | **Summer 1990** 3 months | **School Year 1990-91** 9 months |
|---|---|---|
| **56.** Income earned from work by you | $ .00 | $ .00 |
| **57.** Income earned from work by your spouse | $ .00 | $ .00 |
| **58.** Other taxable income | $ .00 | $ .00 |
| **59.** Nontaxable income and benefits | $ .00 | $ .00 |

**Section L — Student's Expected Other Veterans Benefits**
(July 1, 1990 – June 30, 1991)

**60.** Other benefits administered by the Veterans Administration
(Read page 10 of instructions. Don't include any benefits you already reported in **42** or **43**.)

Amount per month $ .00 Number of months |_|_|

**Section M — Family Members' Listing** Give information for all family members included in **18** or **20**. You are already listed on line 1. List up to seven other family members here. If more than seven, list first those who will be in college at least half-time. List those over seven in Section P.

**61.**

| | Full name of family member | Age | Relationship (Use code below.) | Will attend college at least half-time in 1990-91 school year? Yes | No | Name of school or college this person will attend in 1990-91 school year | Year in school 1990-91 | Occupation of this person |
|---|---|---|---|---|---|---|---|---|
| 1 | **You — the Student Applicant** | | | | | | | |
| 2 | | | | 1☐ | 2☐ | | | |
| 3 | | | | 1☐ | 2☐ | | | |
| 4 | | | | 1☐ | 2☐ | | | |
| 5 | | | | 1☐ | 2☐ | | | |
| 6 | | | | 1☐ | 2☐ | | | |
| 7 | | | | 1☐ | 2☐ | | | |
| 8 | | | | 1☐ | 2☐ | | | |

**Write in the correct code from the right.** 1 = Student's parent 2 = Student's stepparent 3 = Student's brother or sister 4 = Student's husband or wife 5 = Student's son or daughter 6 = Student's grandparent 7 = Other (Explain in Section P.)

**Section N — Parents' Other Information**

**62.** Enter the total sum of losses reported in 1989 from business, farm, capital investments, rents, royalties, partnerships, estates, trusts, pensions, annuities, etc. (1989 IRS Form 1040 — lines 12, 13, 15, 16b, 17b, 18, and 19) $ .00

**63.** If parents own a home, give
**a.** year purchased |1|9|_|_| **b.** purchase price $ .00

07

## Section O — Student's Colleges & Programs

**64.** List the names and CSS code numbers of the colleges and programs to which you want CSS to send information from this form. Give the correct housing code. Don't list the California Student Aid Commission or federal student aid programs. Be sure to include the college(s) you listed in **29**. Enclose the right fee. See the instructions and **65a-b**.

| Name | City and State | CSS Code No. | Housing Code* |
|---|---|---|---|
| | | | |
| | | | |
| | | | |
| | | | |
| | | | |
| | | | |
| | | | |
| | | | |

***Housing Codes for 1990-91** (Enter only one code for each college.):
1 = With parents 2 = Campus housing 3 = Off-campus housing 4 = With relatives

**65. a. Fee:** Mark the box that tells how many colleges and programs are listed in **64**.

CSS Only

1 ☐ **$8.75** 3 ☐ **$22.25** 5 ☐ **$35.75** 7 ☐ **$49.25**
2 ☐ **$15.50** 4 ☐ **$29.00** 6 ☐ **$42.50** 8 ☐ **$56.00**

CSS Use Only

**b. California Student Aid Commission**: If you want to apply for a Cal Grant or Graduate Fellowship, you must:

- mark the box below that applies to you,
- list at least one college in **64**, and
- add **$2.50** to the amount marked in **65a**.

Mark only one box:

1 ☐ I am applying for a new Cal Grant or a new Graduate Fellowship. (Complete Section Q.)

2 ☐ I am a current Cal Grant recipient applying for a Graduate Fellowship. (Complete Section Q.)

3 ☐ I am now receiving a Cal Grant, Bilingual Teacher Grant, or Graduate Fellowship and am applying for a renewal of my grant. (Skip Section Q.)

If you mark a box in **65b**, add $2.50 to the amount in **65a**. For example, if two colleges are listed in **64** ($15.50) and you marked one of the boxes above ($2.50), enclose $18.00. **Mail this form with a check or money order for the right amount made out to the CSS. This form will be returned to you if no fee is enclosed.**

## Section P — Explanations/Special Circumstances

Use this space to explain any special circumstances, unusual expenses, child care expenses, expenses related to the student's disabilities, and/or educational and other debts.

CSS Use Only
1 5 6

**Note:** If you have not already done so, be certain to complete Sections F through P.

## Section Q — New Cal Grant and State Graduate Fellowship Applicants Only:

07

**You (the student) must complete this section and file this form by March 2, 1990, to be considered for a new Cal Grant or a new Graduate Fellowship from the California Student Aid Commission.** Failure to complete the required questions below will result in your not being considered for a Cal Grant or a Graduate Fellowship. Read pages 10-11 of the instructions before completing this section. New Cal Grant applicants must answer **66a.1** and, if applicable, **66a.2**. Applicants should also answer **67**, **68**, **69**, and **70**. Graduate Fellowship applicants must answer **66b.1** and **b.2**, **67**, **68**, and **69**.

**66.** College or School Preference — Cal Grant applicants complete **a.1** and, if applicable, **a.2**. Graduate Fellowship applicants complete **b.1** and **b.2**. Write in the CSS code number for the college or school that you will most likely attend in the fall of 1990. The list of code numbers for eligible institutions starts on page 13.

**a.1 Cal Grant — New Applicants** — College Code

**a.2** If you entered a California community college number in **a.1** and plan to enroll eventually at a four-year or private two-year college, **also** write in the CSS code number for the school or college to which you will transfer and the housing code for that school. (See **64** for housing codes.) — College Code; Housing Code

**b.1 Graduate Fellowship — New Applicants** (Don't complete if you answer **a.1** above.) — College Code

**b.2** Write in the Competition Number of the area in which you wish to compete. (See page 10 for Competition Numbers.) — Competition Number

**67.** Will you have been a resident of California for **at least** one year by September 20, 1990? (See instructions.) Yes ☐1 No ☐2

**68.** Enter your cumulative grade point average (GPA) to two decimal places on a 4.00 scale. (See instructions. GPAs of qualifying students will be verified prior to payment.) __ . __ __

**69.** Complete for both parents/legal guardians, even if one or both are dead or parents are separated, or divorced.

**a.** Father's/legal guardian's highest level of education (Mark only one box.)
1 ☐ None or unknown 2 ☐ Elementary 3 ☐ High School 4 ☐ College

**b.** Mother's/legal guardian's highest level of education (Mark only one box.)
1 ☐ None or unknown 2 ☐ Elementary 3 ☐ High School 4 ☐ College

**70.** To be completed by new Cal Grant applicants only.
Will you have completed more than one semester/two quarters of full-time study, or the equivalent of 16 semester units of part-time study, or more than four and one-half months at a vocational/technical school prior to June 30, 1990? Don't count any noncredit ESL (English as a Second Language) classes you have completed. Yes ☐1 No ☐2

**71.** COMPLETION OF THE FOLLOWING QUESTION IS OPTIONAL. Your voluntary response will not be considered when establishing your eligibility for financial aid. Your response to the question will be used by the Student Aid Commission only for research purposes. Individual respondents will not be identified. Your response will not be sent to the colleges and programs listed in **64** above.

What is your race/ethnic origin?

1 ☐ Black, Negro, African American
2 ☐ Chicano, Mexican American
3 ☐ Latino, other Hispanic
4 ☐ Filipino
5 ☐ Pacific Islander
6 ☐ Vietnamese, Cambodian, Laotian, other Indo-Chinese
7 ☐ Chinese, Japanese, Korean, other Asian
8 ☐ American Indian or Alaskan Native
9 ☐ White, Caucasian
0 ☐ Other

# Family Financial Statement (FFS) 1991-92

**AMERICAN COLLEGE TESTING PROGRAM (ACT)**

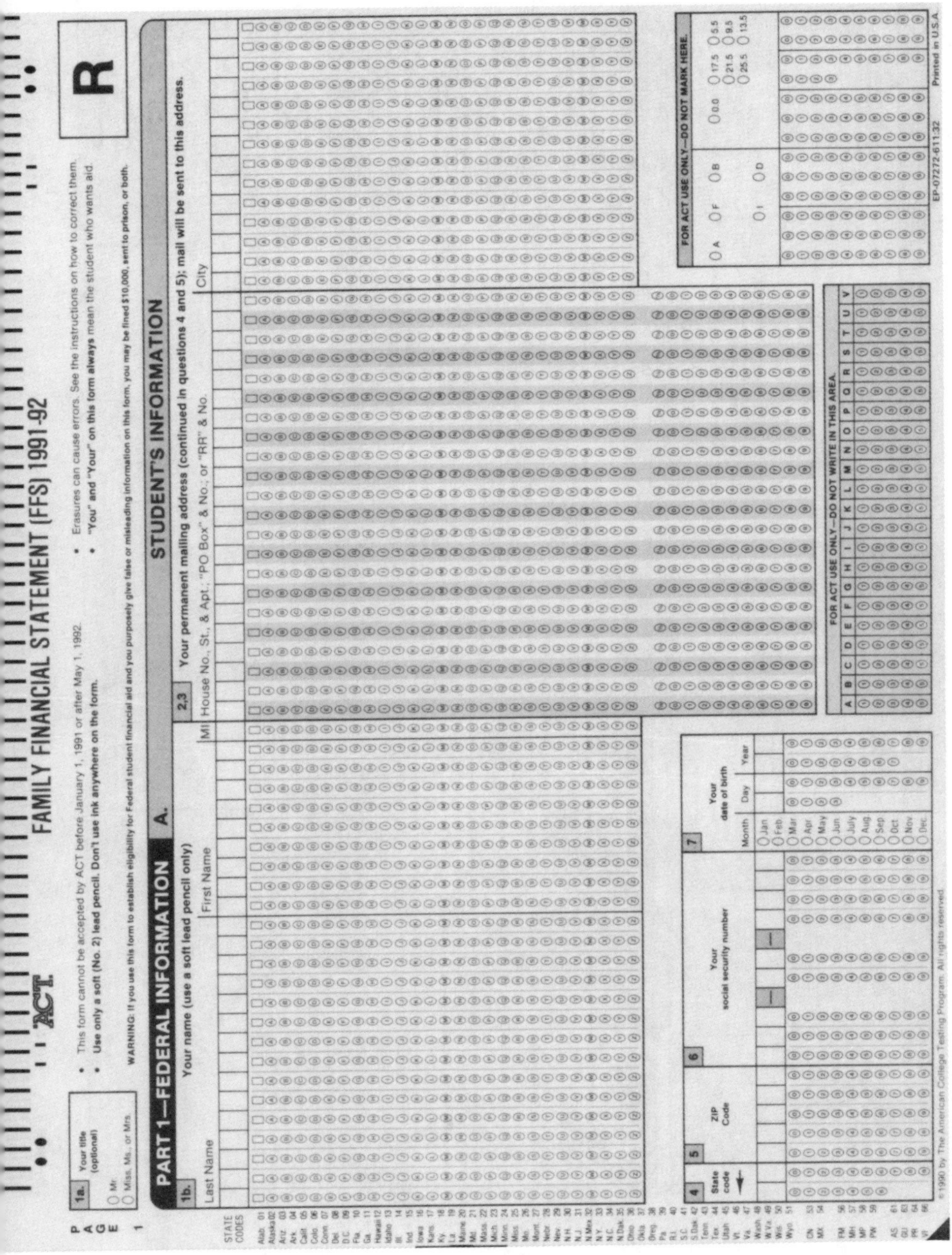
ACT

FAMILY FINANCIAL STATEMENT (FFS) 1991-92

R

PAGE 1

1a. Your title (optional)
- Mr.
- Miss, Ms., or Mrs.

- This form cannot be accepted by ACT before January 1, 1991 or after May 1, 1992.
- **Use only a soft (No. 2) lead pencil. Don't use ink anywhere on the form.**
- Erasures can cause errors. See the instructions on how to correct them.
- **"You" and "Your" on this form always** mean the student who wants aid.

**WARNING: If you use this form to establish eligibility for Federal student financial aid and you purposely give false or misleading information on this form, you may be fined $10,000, sent to prison, or both.**

**PART 1—FEDERAL INFORMATION** **A.** **STUDENT'S INFORMATION**

**1b.** Your name (use a soft lead pencil only)

Last Name | First Name | MI

**2,3** Your permanent mailing address (continued in questions 4 and 5); mail will be sent to this address.

House No., St., & Apt.; "PO Box" & No.; or "RR" & No. | City

STATE CODES

Alab. 01, Alaska 02, Ariz. 03, Ark. 04, Calif. 05, Colo. 06, Conn. 07, Del. 08, D.C. 09, Fla. 10, Ga. 11, Hawaii 12, Idaho 13, Ill. 14, Ind. 15, Iowa 16, Kans. 17, Ky. 18, La. 19, Maine 20, Md. 21, Mass. 22, Mich. 23, Minn. 24, Miss. 25, Mo. 26, Mont. 27, Nebr. 28, Nev. 29, N.H. 30, N.J. 31, N.Mex. 32, N.Y. 33, N.C. 34, N.Dak. 35, Ohio 36, Okla. 37, Oreg. 38, Pa. 39, R.I. 40, S.C. 41, S.Dak. 42, Tenn. 43, Tex. 44, Utah 45, Vt. 46, Va. 47, Wash. 48, W.Va. 49, Wis. 50, Wyo. 51, CN 53, MX 54, FM 56, MH 57, MP 58, PW 59, AS 61, GU 63, PR 64, VI 66

**4** State code ←

**5** ZIP Code

**6** Your social security number

**7** Your date of birth

Month | Day | Year

Jan, Feb, Mar, Apr, May, Jun, July, Aug, Sep, Oct, Nov, Dec

FOR ACT USE ONLY—DO NOT WRITE IN THIS AREA.

A B C D E F G H I J K L M N O P Q R S T U V

FOR ACT USE ONLY—DO NOT MARK HERE.

A F B I D 0.0 17.5 21.5 25.5 5.5 9.5 13.5



EP-07272-611:32 Printed in U.S.A.

PAGE 2

DO NOT STAPLE OR USE TAPE ON THIS FORM

## A. STUDENT'S INFORMATION CONTINUED

**8** Are you a U.S. citizen? (mark only one)

- a. Yes, I am a U.S. citizen.
- b. No, but I am an eligible noncitizen. (See instructions on page 3.)
- c. No, neither of the above. (See instructions on page 3.)

**9** Alien Registration Number (eligible noncitizens only)

A

**10** As of today, are you married? (mark only one)

- I am not married. (I am single, divorced, or widowed.)
- I am married.
- I am separated from my spouse.

**11** Enter your state of legal residence

See state code listing on page 1, left margin.

State Code

**12** What year will you be in college in 1991-92? (mark only one)

- 1st year (never previously attended college)
- 1st year (previously attended college)
- 2nd year
- 3rd year
- 4th year
- 5th year or more (undergraduate)
- 1st year graduate or professional (beyond a Bachelor's degree)
- Continuing graduate or professional

**13** Will you have your first Bachelor's degree before July 1, 1991?

- Yes
- No

## B. Student's Status—READ THE INSTRUCTIONS BEFORE ANSWERING THESE QUESTIONS.

**14a.** Were you born before January 1, 1968? Yes / No

**14b.** Are you a veteran of the U.S. Armed Forces? Yes / No

**14c.** Are you a ward of the court or are both your parents dead? Yes / No

**14d.** Do you have legal dependents *(other than a spouse)* that fit the definition in the instructions on page 4? Yes / No

If you answered **"Yes"** to **any** question in 14, go directly to Section C, question 23. (Skip questions 15 through 22.) Do not complete page 3.

If you answered **"No"** to **all** of the questions in 14 **and** you are:

- Unmarried now (single, divorced, separated, or widowed) **and** will be an undergraduate student in 1991-92, go on to question 15.
- Married now **or** will be a graduate/professional student in 1991-92, go directly to question 22. (Skip questions 15 through 21.)

## Unmarried (single, divorced, separated, or widowed) Undergraduate Students Only

**15** Did your parents claim you as an income tax exemption:

in 1989? Yes / No   in 1990? Yes / No

If you answered **"Yes"** to **either** year in question 15, go directly to Section D, question 25. (Skip the rest of this page.)

If you answered **"No"** to **both** years in question 15, go on to question 16.

**16** Beginning with the 1987-88 school year, you first received Federal student aid. . . (mark only one)

- a. in the 1987-88 school year (go to question 17).
- b. in the 1988-89 school year (go to question 18).
- c. in the 1989-90 school year (go to question 19).
- d. in the 1990-91 school year (go to question 20).
- e. None of the above (go to question 21).

**17** Did you have total resources of $4,000 or more, not including parents' support:

in 1985? Yes / No   in 1986? Yes / No

If you answered **"Yes"** to **both** years in question 17, go directly to Section C, question 23. (Skip questions 18, 19, 20, 21, and 22.) Do not complete page 3 of this form.

If you answered **"No"** to **either** year in question 17, go directly to page 3, question 25. (Skip the rest of this page.)

**18** Did you have total resources of $4,000 or more, not including parents' support:

in 1986? Yes / No   in 1987? Yes / No

If you answered **"Yes"** to **both** years in question 18, go directly to Section C, question 23. (Skip questions 19, 20, 21, and 22.) Do not complete page 3 of this form.

If you answered **"No"** to **either** year in question 18, go directly to page 3, question 25. (Skip the rest of this page.)

## B. Unmarried Undergraduate Students (Continued)

**19** Did you have total resources of $4,000 or more, not including parents' support:

in 1987? Yes / No   in 1988? Yes / No

If you answered **"Yes"** to **both** years in question 19, go directly to Section C, question 23. (Skip questions 20, 21, and 22.) Do not complete page 3 of this form.

If you answered **"No"** to **either** year in question 19, go directly to page 3, question 25. (Skip the rest of this page.)

**20** Did you have total resources of $4,000 or more, not including parents' support:

in 1988? Yes / No   in 1989? Yes / No

If you answered **"Yes"** to **both** years in question 20, go directly to Section C, question 23. (Skip questions 21 and 22.) Do not complete page 3 of this form.

If you answered **"No"** to **either** year in question 20, go directly to page 3, question 25. (Skip the rest of this page.)

**21** Did you have total resources of $4,000 or more, not including parents' support:

in 1989? Yes / No   in 1990? Yes / No

If you answered **"Yes"** to **both** years in question 21, go directly to Section C, question 23. (Skip question 22.) Do not complete page 3 of this form.

If you answered **"No"** to **either** year in question 21, go directly to page 3, question 25. (Skip the rest of this page.)

## Married/Graduate/Professional Only

**22** Will your parents claim you as an income tax exemption in 1991?

Yes / No

If you answered **"Yes"** to question 22, go directly to Section D, question 25. (Skip the rest of this page.)

If you answered **"No"** to question 22, go on to Section C, question 23. Do not complete page 3 of this form.

## C. Student's (& Spouse's) General Info.

**23** Number of family members in 1991-92

Mark the total number of people that you will support in 1991-92. **Always** include yourself (the student) and your spouse. Include your children and other people only if they meet the definition in the instructions on page 4.

**24** Number of college students in 1991-92

Of the number in question 23, mark the number of family members who will be in college at least half-time. Include yourself (the student).

**Skip page 3; go on to page 4, question 39.**

PAGE 3 DO NOT SEND YOUR TAX FORMS TO ACT

FOR OFFICE USE ONLY

1821092

## D. PARENTS' GENERAL INFORMATION

**If your parents have divorced or separated, if your parent is widowed or single, or if you have a stepparent, you must read the instructions for Section D before going on.**

25 What is your parents' current marital status?

- ○ Single
- ○ Married
- ○ Separated
- ○ Divorced
- ○ Widowed

26 What is your parents' state of legal residence? (See list on page 1, left margin.)

27 Number of family members in 1991-92

Mark the total number of people that your parents will support in 1991-92. Always include yourself (the student) and your parents. Include your parents' other children and other people only if they meet the definition in the instructions on page 5.

28 Number of college students in 1991-92

Of the number in question 27, mark the number of family members who will be in college at least half-time. Include yourself (the student).

## E. PARENTS' INCOME INFORMATION FOR 1990— (You must see the instructions for income and taxes that you should exclude from questions 31 through 38.)

29 The following 1990 U.S. income tax figures (questions 30-32) are: (mark only one)

- ○ From a completed 1990 IRS Form 1040EZ or 1040A
- ○ From a completed 1990 IRS Form 1040
- ○ Estimated—will file a 1990 IRS Form 1040EZ or 1040A
- ○ Estimated—will file a 1990 IRS Form 1040
- ○ A tax return will not be filed. (Go to question 33; skip questions 30 through 32.)

**Don't write in cents in the following questions; round all figures to whole U.S. dollars. (Example: If your total 1990 U.S. income tax paid was $3,448.36, you should enter only 3448.)**

**If your answer is zero, put a zero in the right-hand box. Don't leave the question blank.**

You must read the instructions to find the correct 1990 IRS Form 1040, 1040A, or 1040EZ lines for questions 30 through 32. Don't guess! The answers may be different than you think!

30 1990 Total number of exemptions

31 1990 Adjusted Gross Income (AGI) (Read the instructions for question 31 on page 5.) $ .00

32 1990 U.S. income tax paid $ .00

33,34 1990 income earned from work by: Father $ .00 Mother $ .00

**For questions 35 through 38, enter 1990 Untaxed Income & Benefits (yearly totals only).**

35 Social security benefits $ .00

36 Aid to Families with Dependent Children (AFDC or ADC) $ .00

37 Child support received for all children $ .00

38 Other untaxed income & benefits (Use worksheet #2 in the instructions on page 12.) $ .00

PAGE 4 DO NOT SEND YOUR TAX FORMS TO ACT

## F. STUDENT'S (& SPOUSE'S) INCOME INFORMATION FOR 1990—All students must complete this page.

(You must see the instructions for income and taxes that you should exclude from questions 41 through 48.)

**39** The following 1990 U.S. income tax figures (questions 40-42) are: (mark only one)

- ○ From a completed 1990 IRS Form 1040EZ or 1040A
- ○ From a completed 1990 IRS Form 1040
- ○ Estimated—will file a 1990 IRS Form 1040EZ or 1040A
- ○ Estimated—will file a 1990 IRS Form 1040
- ○ A tax return will not be filed. (Go to question 43; skip questions 40 through 42.)

**Don't write in cents in the following questions; round all figures to whole U.S. dollars. (Example: If your total 1990 U.S. income tax paid was $3,448.36, you should enter only 3448.)**

**If your answer is zero, put a zero in the right-hand box. Don't leave the question blank.**

**You must read the instructions to find the correct 1990 IRS Form 1040, 1040A, or 1040EZ lines for questions 40 through 42. Don't guess! The answers may be different than you think!**

| 40 1990 Total number of exemptions | 41 1990 Adjusted Gross Income (AGI) (Read the instructions for question 41 on page 6.) | 42 1990 U.S. income tax paid |
|---|---|---|
| | $ .00 | $ .00 |

**43,44** 1990 Income earned from work by:

| Student | Spouse |
|---|---|
| $ .00 | $ .00 |

1990 Untaxed Income and Benefits (yearly totals only)

| 45 Social security benefits | 46 Aid to Families with Dependent Children (AFDC or ADC) | 47 Child support received for all children | 48 Other untaxed income & benefits (Use worksheet #2 in the instructions on page 12.) |
|---|---|---|---|
| $ .00 | $ .00 | $ .00 | $ .00 |

## G. FEDERAL STUDENT AID RELEASE

**49**

**a. Do you give ACT permission to send information from this FFS to the U.S. Department of Education? (Answer "Yes" if you want to be considered for a Pell Grant and other Federal student financial aid.)**

○ Yes ○ No

**Note:** Answer "Yes" if you want ACT to send information from this FFS to the U.S. Department of Education. If you leave this question blank, we will count it as "No."

**b. Do you give the U.S. Department of Education permission to send family and financial information from this FFS to the financial aid agencies in your state?**

○ Yes ○ No

**Note:** By answering "Yes" you are not applying for state aid in some states. Some agencies that use the FFS also require that you have an ACT report sent to them. (See instructions on page 6.)

**c. Do you give the U.S. Department of Education permission to send family and financial information from this FFS to the college(s) (or its representative) listed in question 50?**

○ Yes ○ No

**Note:** By answering "Yes" you are not applying for college aid in some states. Some colleges that use the FFS also require that you have an ACT report sent to them. (See instructions on page 7.)

**d. Mark this oval if you give the Selective Service permission to register you.**

○

**Note:** If you wish to register with Selective Service using this form, you must answer "Yes" to question 49a. (See instructions on page 7.)

## G. COLLEGE RELEASE

**50** What college(s) do you plan to go to in 1991-92? (See the ACT code listing in the instruction booklet.)

| 1st College choice | 2nd College choice | 3rd College choice |
|---|---|---|
| | | |

## Certification and Signatures—(Everyone giving information on this form must sign below. If you don't sign this form, it will be returned unprocessed.)

**51** **Signature:** Read Certification at right before signing. **The student must sign.** If page 3 is filled out, **at least one parent must also sign.** Blacken the oval next to each person's signature. Sign in pencil.

○ STUDENT'S SIGNATURE

○ STUDENT'S SPOUSE'S SIGNATURE

○ FATHER'S SIGNATURE

○ MOTHER'S SIGNATURE

**CERTIFICATION:** All of the information on this form and the Supplemental Information pages, if completed, is true and complete to the best of my knowledge. If asked by an authorized official, I agree to give proof of the information that I have given on this form and the Supplemental Information pages, if completed. I realize that this proof may include a copy of my U.S., state, or local income tax return. I also realize that if I do not give proof when asked, the student may be denied aid.

**52** The date this form was completed

| Month | Day | Year |
|---|---|---|
| ○ Jan ○ Feb ○ Mar ○ Apr ○ May ○ Jun ○ July ○ Aug ○ Sep ○ Oct ○ Nov ○ Dec | | ○ 91 ○ 92 Don't complete before Jan. 1, 1991. |

**IMPORTANT**

**You must read the instructions on page 7 in the instruction booklet to see if you need to fill out pages 5-8.**

PAGE 5 SUPPLEMENTAL INFORMATION

## H. PARENTS' EXPENSE AND ASSET INFORMATION

**53** 1990 Medical and dental expenses not paid by insurance — $ .00

**54,55** 1990 Elementary, junior high, & high school tuition paid for dependent children
- Amount paid — $ .00 (Don't include tuition paid for the student.)
- For how many dependent children?

**56** Is either of your parents a displaced homemaker? (See instructions on page 8.)
- ◯ Yes
- ◯ No

**57** The age of your older parent is:

**58** Cash, savings, and checking accounts — $ .00

**59,60** Home (renters write in "0")
- What is it worth today? $ .00
- What is owed on it? $ .00

**61,62** Other real estate and investments
- What is it worth today? $ .00
- What is owed on it? $ .00

**63,64** Business and farm
- What is it worth today? $ .00
- What is owed on it? $ .00

**65** Does any part of question 63 include a farm?
- ◯ Yes
- ◯ No

## I. PARENTS' ESTIMATED INCOME INFORMATION FOR 1991—(You must see the instructions for income and taxes that you should exclude from questions 67 through 71.)

**66** Is either of your parents certified as a dislocated worker by the appropriate agency? (See instructions on page 8.)
- ◯ Yes
- ◯ No

All parents should complete questions 67 through 71.

**67,68** 1991 Income earned from work by:
- Father — $ .00
- Mother — $ .00

**69** 1991 Other taxable income — $ .00

**70** 1991 U.S. income tax to be paid — $ .00

**71** 1991 Nontaxable income & benefits (See instructions on page 8.) — $ .00

PAGE 6 SUPPLEMENTAL INFORMATION

## J. STUDENT'S (& SPOUSE'S) EXPENSE AND ASSET INFORMATION

**Complete questions 72, 73, and 74 only if you completed Section C.**

72 1990 Medical and dental expenses not paid by insurance — $ .00

1990 Elementary, junior high, & high school tuition paid for dependent children
73,74 Amount paid — Don't include tuition paid for the student. $ .00 — For how many dependent children?

75 Are you, or is your spouse, a displaced homemaker? (See instructions on page 9.) — ◯ Yes ◯ No

76 Cash, savings, and checking accounts — $ .00

77,78 Home (renters write in "0") — What is it worth today? $ .00 — What is owed on it? $ .00

79,80 Other real estate and investments — What is it worth today? $ .00 — What is owed on it? $ .00

81,82 Business and farm — What is it worth today? $ .00 — What is owed on it? $ .00

83 Does any part of question 81 include a farm? — ◯ Yes ◯ No

## K. VETERANS EDUC. BENEFITS

Expected income and benefits for July 1, 1991 through June 30, 1992.

84,85 Your veterans Dependents Educational Assistance Program benefits — Amount per month $ .00 — No. of months

86,87 Your Veterans Contributory Benefits (VEAP) (Answer only if you completed Section C.) — Amount per month $ .00 — No. of months

## L. STUDENT'S (& SPOUSE'S) ESTIMATED INCOME INFORMATION FOR 1991— (You must see the instructions for income and taxes that you should exclude from questions 89 through 93.)

88 Are you, or is your spouse, certified as a dislocated worker by the appropriate agency? (See instructions on page 9.) — ◯ Yes ◯ No

All students should complete questions 89 through 93.

89,90 1991 Income earned from work by: Student $ .00 — Spouse $ .00

91 1991 Other taxable income — $ .00

92 1991 U.S. income tax to be paid — $ .00

93 1991 Nontaxable income & benefits (See instructions on page 10.) — $ .00

FOR OFFICE USE ONLY

1821092

PAGE 7

# PART 2—COLLEGE/AGENCY/REPORT INFORMATION

## M. LOAN INFORMATION

**94** Are you in default on an educational loan or do you owe a refund to any Title IV aid program?

- ◯ Yes
- ◯ No

Go to question 95.

**STAFFORD LOAN QUESTIONS** →

**95** For what amount of Stafford Loan do you wish to be considered? (If you do not want a loan, leave blank and go to question 101.)

$ ____ .00

**96** What is the total unpaid balance on all Stafford (GSL) Loan(s)? (If none owed, answer "0" and go to question 101.)

$ ____ .00

Questions 97 through 100 refer to your MOST RECENT Stafford (GSL) Loan.

**97** What is the total unpaid balance of your MOST RECENT Stafford (GSL) Loan?

$ ____ .00

**98** On what date did the loan period begin for your MOST RECENT Stafford (GSL) Loan?

Month: ◯ Jan. ◯ Feb. ◯ March ◯ April ◯ May ◯ June ◯ July ◯ Aug. ◯ Sept. ◯ Oct. ◯ Nov. ◯ Dec.

Year

**99** What was the interest rate on your MOST RECENT Stafford (GSL) Loan?

- ◯ 7%
- ◯ 8%
- ◯ 9%
- ◯ 8%/10%

See instructions.

**100** What was your grade level when you received your MOST RECENT Stafford (GSL) Loan? (mark only one)

- ◯ Correspondence/remedial school
- ◯ First year (freshman)
- ◯ Second year (sophomore)
- ◯ Third year (junior)
- ◯ Fourth year (senior)
- ◯ Fifth year (undergraduate)
- ◯ First year (graduate)
- ◯ Second year (graduate)
- ◯ Third year (graduate)
- ◯ Fourth year (graduate)
- ◯ Beyond fourth year (graduate)

**SLS LOAN QUESTIONS (Supplemental Loans for Students)** →

**101** For what amount of SLS loan do you wish to be considered? (If you do not want a loan, leave blank and go to question 108.)

$ ____ .00

**102** Do you wish to defer principal payments on your SLS loan while you are in school?

- ◯ Yes
- ◯ No (If "No" go to question 104.)

**103** If your lender allows you a choice, what do you want to do about interest payments on your SLS loan?

- ◯ Accrue; Capitalize
- ◯ Periodic Installment Payments

See instructions.

**104** What is the total unpaid balance on all SLS loan(s)? (If none owed, answer "0" and go to question 108.)

$ ____ .00

Questions 105 through 107 refer to your MOST RECENT SLS loan.

**105** What is the total unpaid balance of your MOST RECENT SLS loan?

$ ____ .00

**106** On what date did the loan period begin for your MOST RECENT SLS loan?

Month: ◯ Jan. ◯ Feb. ◯ March ◯ April ◯ May ◯ June ◯ July ◯ Aug. ◯ Sept. ◯ Oct. ◯ Nov. ◯ Dec.

Year

**107** What was your grade level when you received your MOST RECENT SLS loan? (mark only one)

- ◯ Correspondence/remedial school
- ◯ First year (freshman)
- ◯ Second year (sophomore)
- ◯ Third year (junior)
- ◯ Fourth year (senior)
- ◯ Fifth year (undergraduate)
- ◯ First year (graduate)
- ◯ Second year (graduate)
- ◯ Third year (graduate)
- ◯ Fourth year (graduate)
- ◯ Beyond fourth year (graduate)

**108** Lender Code—If questions 95 and 101 are blank, go to question 109. Otherwise, see the instructions for question 108 on page 11.

## N. OTHER STUDENT INFORMATION

**109** List the ACT code numbers below for all colleges that you have attended; if none, leave blank. (See the ACT code listing in the instruction booklet.) If you cannot find an ACT code number for a college you attended, enter zeros (0000) here.

| 1st College code number | 2nd College code number | 3rd College code number | 4th College code number |
|---|---|---|---|
| | | | |

**110** Have you attended additional colleges that you were unable to list in question 109?

- ◯ Yes
- ◯ No

**111** During what terms are you requesting aid? (mark all that apply)

- ◯ Summer 1991
- ◯ Fall 1991
- ◯ Winter quarter 1992
- ◯ Spring 1992
- ◯ Summer 1992
- ◯ Other term

**112** What is your planned enrollment status? (mark only one)

- ◯ Full-time student
- ◯ Three-quarter-time student
- ◯ Half-time student
- ◯ Less than half-time student
- ◯ Correspondence

**113** What type of self-help aid do you wish to be offered? (mark only one)

- ◯ Part-time job only
- ◯ Long-term loan only (including Perkins Loans, Stafford Loans, and other long-term loans)
- ◯ Both loan and work (no preference)
- ◯ Both loan and work (prefer work)
- ◯ Both loan and work (prefer loan)

**Note:** The colleges to which you are applying will assume that you wish to be considered for nonrepayable grants.

**114** If you have dependents other than a spouse, how many will be in the following age groups during 1991-92?

| Ages 0-5 | Ages 6-12 | Ages 13 & over |
|---|---|---|
| | | |

**115,116** Other Veterans Educational Benefits (See instructions.)

| Amount per month | No. of months |
|---|---|
| $ ____ .00 | |

PAGE 8

## O. REMINDERS

**ABOUT COMPLETING THE FFS:**

- Make sure the information on page 1 of the FFS has been entered and the ovals have been blackened accurately. Remember, reports from ACT will be sent to the address you list on page 1.
- Make sure you are considered for all the money for which you qualify. You are encouraged to apply for Federal student aid by answering "Yes" to question 49a.
- Make sure every question has been answered (except those you have been told to skip).
- Make sure there are no notes or stray marks on the FFS and do not write in sections you were told to skip. If you erased any oval, make sure the oval for the correct answer or the zero oval has been blackened in that column. Also, make sure that the correct ovals were blackened for every question you answered.

**ABOUT DEPENDENCY STATUS:**

- Be sure that all student status questions that apply to you on page 2, Section B, have been answered. These questions will determine your dependency status and tell you which sections of the FFS to complete.

**ABOUT CODE NUMBERS:**

- Make sure you have chosen the correct code numbers from the *ACT FFS Instructions and Code Listing Booklet.* Make sure you complete questions 50 and 109. Also, be sure to **repeat** the codes you listed in question 50 again in question 117 if you want ACT reports sent to any colleges/programs.

**ABOUT SIGNATURES:**

- Make sure the required signatures are present in question 51, or the FFS will be returned to you. The student must always sign. If page 3 is completed, at least one parent must sign. If the student is married, the spouse must also sign.

**ABOUT MAILING YOUR FFS TO ACT:**

- Do not send letters, tax forms, college forms, or extra material to ACT. Mail only the completed FFS and fee (if you completed page 8).
- Keep the instruction booklet. You may need to refer to it later.
- Make sure you mail your FFS by regular first class mail. (Special handling such as registered, certified, or express mail will delay processing of your form.)

**ABOUT REPORTS AND FEES:**

- If you answer "Yes" to question 49a., ACT will send you a Student Aid Report (SAR) after your FFS has been processed.
- ACT reports (called CFARs) will be sent to the colleges/programs listed in question 117 if the appropriate fee is submitted.
- ACT will send you a CFAR if you answer "Yes" to question 118 and you submit the appropriate fee.
- ACT will also send you an "ACT Report Request" form which you may use to later request additional or corrected CFARs.
- Make sure you include the correct fee for all reports requested in questions 117 and 118.
- If you complete page 8, remember to complete the "FEES" box (Section Q). This will tell you what fee to enclose.
- Make sure you check the appropriate fee box on the back of the FFS envelope. This will speed up the processing of your FFS.
- Make your personal check or money order payable to ACT. DO NOT send cash or coins.

**ACT is a processing service only. ONLY colleges and/or programs can determine the amounts and types of financial aid for which you may qualify. If you request and pay for reports, ACT will send your colleges/programs an analysis they will use to determine your financial aid.**

## P. REQUEST FOR ACT REPORTS

**117** **If you want ACT reports sent directly to any colleges, agencies or programs, list the ACT code numbers from the instruction booklet. Generally, you will want to include the same college codes you listed on page 4, question 50.**

| 1st Code choice | If 1st code choice is a college, where will you live? (mark one) | 2nd Code choice | If 2nd code choice is a college, where will you live? (mark one) | 3rd Code choice | If 3rd code choice is a college, where will you live? (mark one) | 4th Code choice | If 4th code choice is a college, where will you live? (mark one) |
|---|---|---|---|---|---|---|---|
| ⓪–⑨ | ◯ With parents<br>◯ Campus housing<br>◯ Off campus | ⓪–⑨ | ◯ With parents<br>◯ Campus housing<br>◯ Off campus | ⓪–⑨ | ◯ With parents<br>◯ Campus housing<br>◯ Off campus | ⓪–⑨ | ◯ With parents<br>◯ Campus housing<br>◯ Off campus |

**118** **Do you want to request an ACT report for yourself?**

◯ Yes

**(See instructions on page 11.)**

## Q. FEES

**Complete the boxes below to determine the total fee you need to submit.**

☐ Write in the number of codes you listed in question 117.

\+ ☐ Write in a "1" if you marked "yes" to question 118.

= ☐ Total reports requested.

| Total reports requested | | Pay this amount |
|---|---|---|
| 1 | = | $ 5.50 |
| 2 | = | $ 9.50 |
| 3 | = | $13.50 |
| 4 | = | $17.50 |
| 5 | = | $21.50 |

**(Check the box on the back of the envelope for the total fee you are submitting.)**

## R. Student's Name

**Enter your (the student's) first and last name below.** (Note: This will be used to match the pages of the FFS if they become separated.)

First Name (Please Print) ______________________

Last Name (Please Print) ______________________

**NOTE ABOUT SIGNATURES:** The signatures on page 4 certify that you have read and understand the FFS instruction booklet, and that all of the information on this form, including information provided on pages 5 through 8, is accurate and complete.

# APPLICATION FOR FEDERAL STUDENT AID (AFSA)

U.S. DEPARTMENT OF EDUCATION

STUDENT FINANCIAL ASSISTANCE PROGRAMS

# Application for Federal Student Aid

*1990-91 School Year*

FORM APPROVED
OMB NO. 1840-0110
APP. EXP. 6/30/91

U.S. Department of Education
Student Financial
Assistance Programs

**WARNING: If you purposely give false or misleading information on this form, you may be fined $10,000, sent to prison, or both.**

**"You" and "your" on this form always** mean the student who wants aid.

## Section A: Yourself

1. Your name — Last / First / M.I.

2. Your permanent mailing address (Mail will be sent to this address. See page 2 for State/Country abbreviation.) — Number and Street (Include Apt. No.) / City / State / ZIP Code

3. Your title *(optional)*
   - ❑ Mr.
   - ❑ Miss, Ms., or Mrs.

4. Your State of legal residence — State

5. Your social security number

6. Your date of birth — Month / Day / Year

7. Are you a U.S. citizen?
   - ❑ Yes, I am a U.S. citizen.
   - ❑ No, but I am an eligible noncitizen. *(See the instructions on page 2.)* A
   - ❑ No, neither of the above. *(See the instructions on page 3.)*

8. As of **today**, are you married? *(Check only one box.)*
   - ❑ I am not married. (I am single, divorced, or widowed.)
   - ❑ I am married.
   - ❑ I am separated from my spouse.

9. What year will you be in college in 1990-91? *(Check only one box.)*
   - ❑ 1st *(never previously attended college)*
   - ❑ 1st *(previously attended college)*
   - ❑ 2nd ❑ 3rd ❑ 4th
   - ❑ 5th or more undergraduate
   - ❑ first year graduate/professional (beyond a bachelor's degree)
   - ❑ Continuing graduate or professional

10. Will you have your first Bachelor's degree before July 1, 1990?
    ❑ Yes ❑ No

## Section B: Student Status

| 11. | | Yes | No |
|---|---|---|---|
| a. | Were you born **before** January 1, 1967? | ❑ | ❑ |
| b. | Are you a veteran of the U.S. Armed Forces? | ❑ | ❑ |
| c. | Are you a ward of the court or are both your parents dead? | ❑ | ❑ |
| d. | Do you have legal dependents (*other than a spouse*) that fit the definition in the instructions on page 3? | ❑ | ❑ |

If you answered **"Yes"** to **any** part of question 11, go to Section C and fill out the **GRAY** and the **WHITE** areas on the rest of the form. Skip questions 12 through 15.

If you answered **"No"** to **every** part of question 11, **and** you are:

- Unmarried now (single, divorced, separated, or widowed) **and** will be an undergraduate student in 1990-91, answer question 12. (Skip question 15.)
- Married now **or** will be a graduate/professional student in 1990-91, answer question 15. (Skip questions 12 through 14d.)

### Unmarried Undergraduate Students Only

12. Did your parents claim you as an income tax exemption?

| | Yes | No |
|---|---|---|
| . . . in 1988? | ❑ | ❑ |
| . . . in 1989? | ❑ | ❑ |

If you answered **"Yes"** to **either** year in question 12, go to Section C, and fill out the **BLUE** and the **WHITE** areas on the rest of the form. (Skip questions 13 through 15.)

If you answered **"No"** to **both** years in question 12, answer question 13 below.

13. **Beginning with the 1987-88 school year,** you **first** received Federal student aid...***(Check only one box: a, b, c, or d. See instructions on page 3.)***

**a.** ❑ In the 1987-88 school year. (Answer **14a below.** Skip questions 14b, 14c, and 14d.)

**b.** ❑ In the 1988-89 school year. (Answer **14b below.** Skip questions 14a, 14c, and 14d.)

**c.** ❑ In the 1989-90 school year. (Answer **14c below.** Skip questions 14a, 14b, and 14d.)

**d.** ❑ In neither a, b, **or** c. (Answer **14d below.** Skip questions 14a, 14b, and 14c.)

**14a.** Did you have total resources of $4,000 or more, not including parents' support?

| | Yes | No |
|---|---|---|
| . . . in 1985? | ❑ | ❑ |
| . . . in 1986? | ❑ | ❑ |

**14b.** Did you have total resources of $4,000 or more, not including parents' support?

| | Yes | No |
|---|---|---|
| . . . in 1986? | ❑ | ❑ |
| . . . in 1987? | ❑ | ❑ |

**14c.** Did you have total resources of $4,000 or more, not including parents' support?

| | Yes | No |
|---|---|---|
| . . . in 1987? | ❑ | ❑ |
| . . . in 1988? | ❑ | ❑ |

**14d.** Did you have total resources of $4,000 or more, not including parents' support?

| | Yes | No |
|---|---|---|
| . . . in 1988? | ❑ | ❑ |
| . . . in 1989? | ❑ | ❑ |

- If you answered **"No"** to **either** year in question 14a, 14b, 14c, **or** 14d, go to Section C and fill out the **BLUE** and the **WHITE** areas on the rest of the form.
- If you answered **"Yes"** to **both** years in question 14a, 14b, 14c, **or** 14d, go to Section C and fill out the **GRAY** and the **WHITE** areas on the rest of the form.

### Married or Graduate/Professional Students Only

15. Will your parents claim you as an income tax exemption in 1990?

| Yes | No |
|---|---|
| ❑ | ❑ |

If you answered **"Yes"** to question 15, go to Section C and fill out the **BLUE** and the **WHITE** areas on the rest of the form.

If you answered **"No"** to question 15, go to Section C and fill out the **GRAY** and the **WHITE** areas on the rest of the form.

**ED FORM 255**

## Section C: Household Information

**PARENTS**

**16.** What is your parents' current marital status?

- ❑ unmarried (single, divorced, or widowed)
- ❑ married
- ❑ separated

**17.** What is your parents' State of legal residence?

|__|__|
State

**18.** Number of family members in 1990-91 |__|__|

(Write in the total number of people that your parents will support in 1990-91. Always include yourself and your parents. Include your parents' other children and other people only if they meet the definition in the instructions on page 4.)

**19.** Number of college students in 1990-91 |__|

(Of the number in 18, write in the number of family members who will be in college at least half-time. Include yourself.)

**STUDENT (& SPOUSE)**

**20.** Number of family members in 1990-91 |__|__|

(Write in the total number of people that you will support in 1990-91. Always include yourself and your spouse. Include your children and other people only if they meet the definition in the instructions on page 4.)

**21.** Number of college students in 1990-91 |__|

(Of the number in 20, write in the number of family members who will be in college at least half-time. Include yourself.)

## Section D: 1989 income, earnings, and benefits

*(You **must** see the instructions for income and taxes that you should exclude from questions 24 through 28.)*

**22.** The following 1989 U.S. income tax figures are from....

**Everyone must fill out the Student (& Spouse) column below.**

**PARENTS**
*(Check only one box.)*

- ❑ a completed 1989 IRS Form 1040EZ or 1040A (Go to 23.)
- ❑ a completed 1989 IRS Form 1040 (Go to 23.)
- ❑ an estimated 1989 IRS Form 1040EZ or 1040A (Go to 23.)
- ❑ an estimated 1989 IRS Form 1040 (Go to 23.)
- ❑ a tax return will not be filed. (Skip to 26.)

**STUDENT (& SPOUSE)**
*(Check only one box.)*

- ❑ a completed 1989 IRS Form 1040EZ or 1040A (Go to 23.)
- ❑ a completed 1989 IRS Form 1040 (Go to 23.)
- ❑ an estimated 1989 IRS Form 1040EZ or 1040A (Go to 23.)
- ❑ an estimated 1989 IRS Form 1040 (Go to 23.)
- ❑ a tax return will not be filed. (Skip to 26.)

**TAX FILERS ONLY**

| | Parents | | Student (& Spouse) |
|---|---|---|---|
| **23.** 1989 total number of exemptions (Form 1040-line 6e, or 1040A-line 6e; 1040EZ filers, see instructions on pages 5 and 6.) | \|__\|__\| | **23.** | \|__\|__\| |
| **24.** 1989 income from IRS Form 1040-line 31, 1040A-line 13, or 1040EZ-line 3, or see instructions on pages 5 and 6. | $________.00 | **24.** | $________.00 |
| **25.** 1989 U.S. income tax paid (Form 1040-line 47, 1040A-line 22, or 1040EZ-line 7) | $________.00 | **25.** | $________.00 |

| | | | | |
|---|---|---|---|---|
| **26.** 1989 income earned from work | Father | $________.00 | Student **26.** | $________.00 |
| **27.** 1989 income earned from work | Mother | $________.00 | Spouse **27.** | $________.00 |

**28.** 1989 untaxed income and benefits *(**yearly totals only**)* — **28.**

| | Parents | | Student (& Spouse) |
|---|---|---|---|
| **a.** Social security benefits | $________.00 | **a.** | $________.00 |
| **b.** Aid to Families with Dependent Children (AFDC or ADC) | $________.00 | **b.** | $________.00 |
| **c.** Child support received for all children | $________.00 | **c.** | $________.00 |
| **d.** Other untaxed income and benefits from worksheet #2 on page 11. | $________.00 | **d.** | $________.00 |

## Section E: College Release and Certification

**29.** What college(s) do you plan to go to in 1990-91?

| | College Name | Street Address | City | State |
|---|---|---|---|---|
| a. | | | | |
| b. | | | | |

**30.** Do you give the U.S. Dept. of Education permission to send information from this form to:

**a.** The financial aid agency in your State?

❑ Yes
❑ No

**b.** The college(s) you named in 29 (or its representative)?

❑ Yes
❑ No

**31.** ❑ Check this box if you give Selective Service permission to register you. *(See instructions on page 6.)*

Dept. of Ed Use Only
*(Do not write in this box.)*

**32. Read and sign**

**Certification:** All of the information on this form and the Supplemental Information page, if completed, is true and complete to the best of my knowledge. If asked by an authorized official, I agree to give proof of the information that I have given on this form and the Supplemental Information page, if completed. I realize that this proof may include a copy of my U.S., State, or local income tax return. I also realize that if I do not give proof when asked, the student may be denied aid.

Student

Student's spouse

Father

Mother

Date completed Month Day Year ❑ 1990 ❑ 1991

## ATTENTION

**If you are filling out the BLUE and WHITE areas, you will need to refer to Section D to complete worksheet #3A below. The worksheet will tell you whether you must fill out the Supplemental Information (Sections F through I).**

### WORKSHEET #3A FOR THE SIMPLIFIED NEEDS TEST

**1.** Did or will you, your spouse, **or** your parents file a 1989 IRS Form 1040?

❑ Yes (Fill out Sections F through I.)
❑ No (Fill out the rest of this worksheet.)

Check "Yes" if a foreign or Puerto Rican tax return was or will be filed.

| **Income from:** | PARENTS COLUMN A | STUDENT/SPOUSE COLUMN B |
|---|---|---|
| **2a.** Question 24 | $________.00 | $________.00 |
| OR | | |
| **2b.** Questions 26 and 27 (use **only** if you left Question 24 blank) | $________.00 | $________.00 |

**3.** Write in the total of column A and column B entries from Question 2. $________.00

If the total from **3** is **$15,000 or less**, mail the form. **You do not have to fill out the Supplemental Information** (unless you, your spouse or at least one of your parents is a dislocated worker or your school or State asks you to). **Mail the form to:** Federal Student Aid Programs, P.O. Box 6367, Princeton, NJ 08541

If the total from **3** is **$15,001 or more**, you **must** fill out Sections F through I.

**If you are filling out the GRAY and WHITE areas, you will need to refer to Section D to complete worksheet #3B below. The worksheet will tell you whether you must fill out the Supplemental Information (Sections F through I).**

### WORKSHEET #3B FOR THE SIMPLIFIED NEEDS TEST

**1.** Did or will you (or your spouse) file a 1989 IRS Form 1040?

❑ Yes (Fill out Sections F through I.)
❑ No (Fill out the rest of this worksheet.)

Check "Yes" if a foreign or Puerto Rican tax return was or will be filed.

| **Income from:** | STUDENT/SPOUSE |
|---|---|
| **2a.** Question 24 | $________.00 |
| OR | OR |
| **2b.** Questions 26 and 27 (use **only** if you left Question 24 blank) | $________.00 |

If the answer from either Question 2a or 2b is **$15,000 or less**, mail the form. **You do not have to fill out the Supplemental Information** (unless you are, or your spouse is a dislocated worker or your school or State asks you to). **Mail the form to:** Federal Student Aid Programs, P.O. Box 6367, Princeton, NJ 08541

If the answer from either Question 2a or 2b is **$15,001 or more**, you **must** fill out Sections F through I.

# SUPPLEMENTAL INFORMATION

## Section F: 1989 expenses

| | PARENTS | STUDENT (& SPOUSE) |
|---|---|---|
| **33.** 1989 medical and dental expenses not paid by insurance | $__________.00 | **33.** $__________.00 |
| **34.** 1989 elementary, junior high, and high school tuition for dependent children | | |
| **a.** Amount paid (Don't include tuition paid for the applicant.) | $__________.00 | **34a.** $__________.00 |
| **b.** For how many dependent children | ☐☐ | **34b.** ☐☐ |

## Section G: Asset Information

**If you are completing this page, you must fill out the student (& spouse) column below.**

| | PARENTS | | STUDENT (& SPOUSE) | |
|---|---|---|---|---|
| **35.** Is either of your parents a displaced homemaker? *(See the instructions on page 7.)* / Are you, or is your spouse, a displaced homemaker? *(See the instructions on page 8.)* | ☐ Yes | ☐ No | ☐ Yes | ☐ No |
| **36.** Write in the age of your older parent. | ☐☐ | | | |
| | **What is it worth today?** | **What is owed on it?** | **What is it worth today?** | **What is owed on it?** |
| **37.** Cash, savings, and checking accounts | $________.00 | XXXXXXXXXX | **37.** $________.00 | XXXXXXXXXX |
| **38.** Home (Renters write in "0.") | $________.00 | $________.00 | **38.** $________.00 | $________.00 |
| **39.** Other real estate and investments | $________.00 | $________.00 | **39.** $________.00 | $________.00 |
| **40.** Business and farm | $________.00 | $________.00 | **40.** $________.00 | $________.00 |
| **41.** Does any part of item 40 include a farm? | ☐ Yes | ☐ No | **41.** ☐ Yes | ☐ No |

## Section H: Your veterans educational benefits per month *(for the student only)*

**(If you are completing this page, you must answer question 42. If you are filling out the GRAY and the WHITE areas, you must also answer question 43.)**

**Expected Amount**
**July 1, 1990 through June 30, 1991**

**42.** Your veterans "old" GI Bill and Dependents Educational Assistance Program benefits

- **a.** Amount per month $__________.00 a month
- **b.** Number of months ☐☐ months

**43.** Your Veterans Contributory Benefits (VEAP)

- **a.** Amount per month $__________.00 a month
- **b.** Number of months ☐☐ months

## Section I: Expected 1990 taxable and nontaxable income and benefits

*(You **must** see the instructions for income and taxes that you should exclude from questions 45 through 49.)*

**If you are completing this page, you must fill out the student (& spouse) column below.**

**PARENTS**

**44.** Is either of your parents **certified** as a dislocated worker by the appropriate agency? *(See the instructions on page 9.)*

☐ Yes (Fill out the rest of this column, and go to the student and spouse column, question 44.)

☐ No (Go to the student and spouse column, question 44.)

**STUDENT (& SPOUSE)**

**44.** Are you, or is your spouse, **certified** as a dislocated worker by the appropriate agency? *(See the instructions on page 9.)*

☐ Yes (Fill out the rest of this column.)

☐ No (Skip this column, and mail the form.)

| | PARENTS | | STUDENT (& SPOUSE) |
|---|---|---|---|
| **45.** 1990 U.S. income tax to be paid | $__________.00 | | **45.** $__________.00 |
| **46.** 1990 income earned from work — Father | $__________.00 | Student | **46.** $__________.00 |
| **47.** 1990 income earned from work — Mother | $__________.00 | Spouse | **47.** $__________.00 |
| **48.** 1990 other taxable income | $__________.00 | | **48.** $__________.00 |
| **49.** 1990 nontaxable income and benefits *(See instructions on page 9.)* | $__________.00 | | **49.** $__________.00 |

STOP

You have finished the application. Recheck your application. **MAKE SURE THAT YOU HAVE COMPLETED SECTION E.**
**Mail the application to:** Federal Student Aid Programs, P.O. Box 6367, Princeton, NJ 08541

# FINANCIAL AID FORM (FAF)

**COLLEGE SCHOLARSHIP BOARD**

**THE COLLEGE BOARD**

**THE COLLEGE ENTRANCE EXAM BOARD**

# FAF® Financial Aid Form — School Year 1990-91

**Warning: If you use this form to establish eligibility for federal student aid and you purposely give false or misleading information, you may be subject to a $10,000 fine, a prison sentence, or both.**

Do not write in this space.

Use only a No. 2 (soft lead) pencil. Don't write outside of the boxes or answer spaces. "You" and "your" on this form always means the student who wants aid.

## Section A — Student's Identification Information

**1.** Your name ______ Last ______ First ______ M.I.

**2.** Your permanent mailing address (Mail will be sent to this address. See page 2 for state/country abbreviation.) ______ Number, street, and apartment number ______ City ______ State ______ Zip Code

**3.** Your title (optional) 1 ☐ Mr. 2 ☐ Miss, Ms., or Mrs.

**4.** Your state of legal residence ______

**5.** Your social security number ___ - __ - ____

**6.** Your date of birth ______ Month ______ Day ______ Year

**7.** Are you a U.S. citizen? (Mark only one box.)

1 ☐ Yes, I am a U.S. citizen.

2 ☐ No, but I am an eligible noncitizen. (See the instructions on page 2.) A ______

3 ☐ No, neither of the above. (See the instructions on page 3.)

**8.** As of today, are you married? (Mark only one box.)

1 ☐ I am not married. (I am single, divorced, or widowed.)

2 ☐ I am married.

3 ☐ I am separated from my spouse.

**9.** What year will you be in college in 1990-91? (Mark only one box.)

1 ☐ 1st (never previously attended college)

2 ☐ 1st (previously attended college)

3 ☐ 2nd

4 ☐ 3rd

5 ☐ 4th

6 ☐ 5th or more undergraduate

7 ☐ first year graduate/professional (beyond a bachelor's degree)

8 ☐ continuing graduate or professional

**10.** Will you have your first bachelor's degree before July 1, 1990? Yes ☐ 1 No ☐

## Section B — Student Status

**11.** a. Were you born **before** January 1, 1967? Yes ☐ 1 No ☐ 2

b. Are you a veteran of the U.S. Armed Forces? Yes ☐ 1 No ☐ 2

c. Are you a ward of the court or are both your parents dead? Yes ☐ 1 No ☐ 2

d. Do you have legal dependents (other than a spouse) that fit the definition in the instructions on page 3? Yes ☐ 1 No ☐ 2

- If you answered "Yes" to any part of question **11**, go to Section C and fill in the **GRAY** and the **WHITE** areas on the rest of the form. Some colleges may also ask you to complete the **BLUE** areas. (Skip questions **12** through **15**.)
- If you answered "No" to every part of question **11** and you are:
  —unmarried now (single, divorced, separated, or widowed) **and** will be an undergraduate student in 1990-91, answer question **12**. (Skip question **15**.)
  —married now or will be a graduate/professional student in 1990-91, answer question **15**. (Skip questions **12** through **14d**.)

### Unmarried Undergraduate Students Only

**12.** Did your parents claim you as an income tax exemption ...in 1988? Yes ☐ 1 No ☐ 2 ...in 1989? Yes ☐ 1 No ☐ 2

- If you answered "Yes" to **either** year in question **12**, go to Section C and fill in the **BLUE** and the **WHITE** areas on the rest of the form. (Skip questions **13** through **15**.)
- If you answered "No" to **both** years in question **12**, answer question **13** below.

**13.** Beginning with the 1987-88 school year, when did you **first** receive federal student financial aid? (Mark only one box. See instructions on page 3.)

1 ☐ During the 1987-88 school year → (Answer **14a** only. Skip questions **14b**, **14c**, and **14d**.)

2 ☐ During the 1988-89 school year → (Answer **14b** only. Skip questions **14a**, **14c**, and **14d**.)

3 ☐ During the 1989-90 school year → (Answer **14c** only. Skip questions **14a**, **14b**, and **14d**.)

4 ☐ In neither 1, nor 2, nor 3. → (Answer **14d** only. Skip questions **14a**, **14b**, and **14c**.)

**14.** a. Did you have total resources of $4,000 or more, not including parents' support ...in 1985? Yes ☐ 1 No ☐ 2 ...in 1986? Yes ☐ 1 No ☐ 2

**14.** b. Did you have total resources of $4,000 or more, not including parents' support ...in 1986? Yes ☐ 1 No ☐ 2 ...in 1987? Yes ☐ 1 No ☐ 2

**14.** c. Did you have total resources of $4,000 or more, not including parents' support ...in 1987? Yes ☐ 1 No ☐ 2 ...in 1988? Yes ☐ 1 No ☐ 2

**14.** d. Did you have total resources of $4,000 or more, not including parents' support ...in 1988? Yes ☐ 1 No ☐ 2 ...in 1989? Yes ☐ 1 No ☐ 2

After you answer **14a**, **14b**, **14c**, or **14d**, follow the instructions at the right.

- If you answered "No" to **either** year in question **14a**, **14b**, **14c**, or **14d**, go to Section C and fill in the **BLUE** and the **WHITE** areas on the rest of the form.
- If you answered "Yes" to **both** years in question **14a**, **14b**, **14c**, or **14d**, go to Section C and fill in the **GRAY** and the **WHITE** areas on the rest of the form. Some colleges may also ask you to complete the **BLUE** areas.

### Married Students or Graduate/Professional Students Only

**15.** Will your parents claim you as an income tax exemption in 1990? Yes ☐ 1 No ☐ 2

- If you answered "Yes" to question **15**, go to Section C and fill in the **BLUE** and the **WHITE** areas on the rest of the form.
- If you answered "No" to question **15**, go to Section C and fill in the **GRAY** and the **WHITE** areas on the rest of the form. Some colleges may also ask you to complete the **BLUE** areas.

## Section C — Household Information

### Parents

**16.** What is your parents' current marital status? (Mark only one box.) 1 ☐ single 2 ☐ married 3 ☐ separated 4 ☐ divorced 5 ☐ widowed

**17.** What is your parents' state of legal residence? ______

**18.** Number of family members in 1990-91 ______
Write in the total number of people your parents will support in 1990-91. **Always include yourself (the student) and your parents.** Include your parents' other children and other people only if they meet the definition in the instructions on page 3.

**19.** Number of college students in 1990-91 ______
Of the number in **18**, write in the number of family members who will be in college at least half-time. Include yourself — the student who is applying for aid.

### Student (and Spouse)

**20.** Number of family members in 1990-91 ______
Write in the total number of people that you will support in 1990-91. Include yourself and your spouse. Include your children and other people only if they meet the definition in the instructions on page 3.

**21.** Number of college students in 1990-91 ______
Of the number in **20**, write in the number of family members who will be in college at least half-time. Include yourself.

**Section D — 1989 Income, Earnings, and Benefits** (You must see the instructions for income and taxes that you should exclude from questions **24** through **28**.)

Everyone must fill out the Student (and Spouse) column below.

| | | Parents | Student (and Spouse) |
|---|---|---|---|
| **22.** The following 1989 U.S. income tax return figures are (Mark only one box.) | from a completed IRS Form 1040EZ or 1040A. (Go to **23.**) | 22. 1 ☐ | 22. 1 ☐ |
| | from a completed IRS Form 1040. (Go to **23.**) | 2 ☐ | 2 ☐ |
| | estimated. Will file IRS Form 1040EZ or 1040A. (Go to **23.**) | 3 ☐ | 3 ☐ |
| | estimated. Will file IRS Form 1040. (Go to **23.**) | 4 ☐ | 4 ☐ |
| | a tax return will not be filed. (Skip to **26.**) | 5 ☐ | 5 ☐ |
| Tax Filers Only **23.** 1989 total number of exemptions (IRS Form 1040 — line 6e, 1040A — line 6e, or 1040EZ — see instructions on page 4) | | 23. ☐☐ | Tax Filers Only 23. ☐☐ |
| **24.** 1989 income from IRS Form 1040 — line 31, 1040A — line 13, or 1040EZ — line 3 (See instructions on page 4.) | | 24. $ .00 | 24. $ .00 |
| **25.** 1989 U.S. income tax paid (IRS Form 1040 — line 47, 1040A — line 22, or 1040EZ — line 7) | | 25. $ .00 | 25. $ .00 |
| **26.** 1989 income earned from work by | Father | 26. $ .00 | Student 26. $ .00 |
| **27.** 1989 income earned from work by | Mother | 27. $ .00 | Spouse 27. $ .00 |
| **28.** 1989 untaxed income and benefits (yearly totals only) | | | |
| a. Social security benefits | | 28a. $ .00 | 28a. $ .00 |
| b. Aid to Families with Dependent Children (AFDC or ADC) | | b. $ .00 | b. $ .00 |
| c. Child support received for all children | | c. $ .00 | c. $ .00 |
| d. Other untaxed 1989 income and benefits from Worksheet II on page 8 of the instructions | | d. $ .00 | d. $ .00 |

**Section E — Federal Student Aid Releases and Certification**

**29.** What college(s) do you plan to go to in 1990-91?

| Name | City and State | CSS Code No. |
|---|---|---|
| | | |
| | | |

**30. a.** Do you give CSS permission to send information from this form to the U.S. Department of Education? (Mark "Yes" if you want to be considered for a Pell Grant and other federal student financial aid. If you answer "No," skip **30b** and **31**.) Yes ☐1 No ☐2

**30. b.** Do you give the U.S. Department of Education permission to send information from this form to:

— the financial aid agency in your state? Yes ☐1 No ☐2

— the college(s) you named in **29** (or its representative)? Yes ☐1 No ☐2

**Note:** By marking "Yes" you are not applying for state and institutional aid in most states. Most agencies and colleges also require that a CSS report be sent to them. See instructions.

**31.** Mark this box if you give Selective Service permission to register you. (See instructions.) ☐

**32. Certification:** All of the information on this form and the Supplemental Information, if completed, is true and complete to the best of my knowledge. If asked by an authorized official, I agree to give proof of the information that I have given on this form and the Supplemental Information, if completed. I realize that this proof may include a copy of my U.S., state, or local income tax return. I also realize that if I don't give proof when asked, the student may be denied aid.

**Everyone giving information on this form must sign below.**

1 ____________ Student's signature

2 ____________ Student's spouse's signature

3 ____________ Father's signature

4 ____________ Mother's signature

**Date this form was completed:**

☐☐ Month ☐☐ Day 1 ☐1990 2 ☐1991 Year

Write in the month and day. Mark the year completed.

**IMPORTANT: You must read the instructions on page 5 to see if you need to fill out Sections F through I.**

## SUPPLEMENTAL INFORMATION

**Section F — 1989 Expenses**

| | Parents | Student (and Spouse) |
|---|---|---|
| **33.** 1989 medical and dental expenses not paid by insurance | 33. $ .00 | 33. $ .00 |
| **34.** 1989 elementary, junior high, and high school tuition for dependent children a. Amount paid (Don't include tuition paid for the applicant.) | 34a. $ .00 | 34a. $ .00 |
| b. For how many dependent children? (Don't include the applicant.) | b. ☐ | b. ☐ |

**Section G — Asset Information**

If you are completing this section, you must fill out the Student (and Spouse) columns below.

| | Parents: What is it worth today? | Parents: What is owed on it? | Student (and Spouse): What is it worth today? | Student (and Spouse): What is owed on it? |
|---|---|---|---|---|
| **35.** Is either of your parents a displaced homemaker? (See instructions on page 5.) / Are you or is your spouse a displaced homemaker? (See instructions on page 6.) | 35. Yes ☐1 No ☐2 | | 35. Yes ☐1 No ☐2 | |
| **36.** Write in the age of your older parent. | 36. ☐☐ | | 36. XXXXXXXXXXXXXXXX | |
| **37.** Cash, savings, and checking accounts | 37. $ .00 | XXXXXXXXXXXXXXX | 37. $ .00 | XXXXXXXXXXXXXXX |
| **38.** Home (Renters write in "0.") | 38. $ .00 | $ .00 | 38. $ .00 | $ .00 |
| **39.** Other real estate and investments | 39. $ .00 | $ .00 | 39. $ .00 | $ .00 |
| **40.** Business and farm | 40. $ .00 | $ .00 | 40. $ .00 | $ .00 |
| **41.** Does any part of **40** include a farm? | 41. Yes ☐1 No ☐2 | | 41. Yes ☐1 No ☐2 | |

**Section H — Student's Veterans Educational Benefits** (Expected Amount July 1, 1990 – June 30, 1991) (If you are completing this section, you must answer question **42**. If you are filling out the gray and white areas, you must also answer question **43**.)

**42.** Your veterans "old" GI Bill & Dependents Educational Assistance Benefits

a. Amount per month $ .00 b. Number of months ☐☐

**43.** Your VA Contributory Benefits (VEAP)

a. Amount per month $ .00 b. Number of months ☐☐

Print your name Last First

## Section I — Expected 1990 Taxable & Nontaxable Income & Benefits

(You must see the instructions for income and taxes that you should exclude from questions **45** through **49**.)

**If you are completing this section, you must fi out the Student (and Spouse) column below.**

**Parents**

**44.** Is either parent **certified** as a dislocated worker by the appropriate agency? (See instructions on page 6.) **44.** Yes 1 No 2

**45.** 1990 U.S. income tax to be paid **45.** $ .00

**46.** 1990 income earned from work by **Father** **46.** $ .00

**47.** 1990 income earned from work by **Mother** **47.** $ .00

**48.** 1990 other taxable income **48.** $ .00

**49.** 1990 nontaxable income and benefits (See instructions on page 6.) **49.** $ .00

**Student (and Spouse)**

Are you or is your spouse **certified** as a dislocated worker by the appropriate agency? (See instructions on page 6.) **44.** Yes 1 No 2

**45.** $ .00

**Student** **46.** $ .00

**Spouse** **47.** $ .00

**48.** $ .00

**49.** $ .00

## Section J — Student's Other Information

**50.** Your home telephone — Area Code — Number

**51.** Date you began living in your state of legal residence Month Year

**52.** If you have dependents other than a spouse, **how many** will be in each of the following age groups during 1990-91? Ages 0-5 Ages 6-12 Ages 13+

**53.** If you are now in high school, give your high school 6-digit code number.

**54. a.** List all colleges or schools that you have attended since high school. Always list first the college or school most recently attended.

| Name, city, and state of college | Period of attendance From (mo./yr.) | To (mo./yr.) | CSS Code Number |
|---|---|---|---|
| | | | |
| | | | |
| | | | |

**b.** If you have attended more than three colleges or schools, mark here. Give names and CSS code numbers in Section R.

**55.** Your course of study code (See instructions.)

**56.** Date you expect to complete your current college degree/certificate Month Year

**57.** Your expected enrollment status during the 1990-91 school year (Mark only one box.)

1 Full-time 2 At least half-time but less than full-time 3 Less than half-time

**58.** During the 1990-91 school year, you want financial aid from Month Year through Month Year

**59.** Mark your preference for work or loan assistance.

1 Part-time job only 3 Loan only
2 Part-time job and loan 4 No preference

**60. a.** Your Occupation/ Employer

**b.** Employer's Address

**c.** Will you continue to work for this employer during the 1990-91 school year? Yes 1 No 2

**61.** Are you currently in default on an educational loan? (See instructions.) Yes 1 No 2

**62.** Do you owe a refund on a federal grant? (See instructions.) Yes 1 No 2

**63. a.** Your driver's license number

**b.** State that issued the above driver's license number State

## Section K — Student's Other Income

(See instructions for the kinds of income to exclude.)

| | Summer 1990 3 months | School Year 1990-91 9 months |
|---|---|---|
| **64.** Income earned from work by you | $ .00 | $ .00 |
| **65.** Income earned from work by your spouse | $ .00 | $ .00 |
| **66.** Other taxable income | $ .00 | $ .00 |
| **67.** Nontaxable income and benefits | $ .00 | $ .00 |

## Section L — Student's Expected Other Veterans Benefits

(July 1, 1990 – June 30, 1991)

**68.** Other benefits administered by the Veterans Administration (Read page 7 of instructions. Don't include any benefits you already reported in **42** or **43**.)

Amount per month $ .00 Number of months

## Section M — Family Members' Listing

Give information for all family members included in **18** or **20**. You are already listed on line 1. List up to seven other family members here. If more than seven, list first those who will be in college at least half-time. List those over seven in Section R.

| **69.** | Full name of family member | Age | Relationship (Use code below.) | Will attend college at least half-time in 1990-91 school year? Yes | No | Name of school or college this person will attend in 1990-91 school year | Year in school 1990-91 | Occupation/Employer of this person | If attended same school in 1989-90, give amount of: 1989-90 Scholarships/Grants | 1989-90 Parents' Contribution |
|---|---|---|---|---|---|---|---|---|---|---|
| 1 | **You — the Student Applicant** | | | | | | | | | |
| 2 | | | | 1 | 2 | | | | | |
| 3 | | | | 1 | 2 | | | | | |
| 4 | | | | 1 | 2 | | | | | |
| 5 | | | | 1 | 2 | | | | | |
| 6 | | | | 1 | 2 | | | | | |
| 7 | | | | 1 | 2 | | | | | |
| 8 | | | | 1 | 2 | | | | | |

**Write in the correct code from the right.**

1 = Student's parent
2 = Student's stepparent
3 = Student's brother or sister
4 = Student's husband or wife
5 = Student's son or daughter
6 = Student's grandparent
7 = Other (Explain in Section R.)

00

**Section N — Parents' Other Information**

**70.** Parents' monthly home mortgage/rental payment (If none, explain in Sect. R.) $ .00

**71.** If parents own a home, give **a.** year purchased 1 9 __ __ **b.** purchase price $ .00

**72.** If parents included investments in **39**, give their worth today. $ .00

**73.** Breakdown of 1989 income in **24** (Tax Filers Only)

**a.** Wages, salaries, tips (IRS 1040—line 7, 1040A—line 7, or 1040EZ—line 1) **a.** $ .00

**b.** Interest income (IRS 1040—line 8a, 1040A—line 8a, or 1040EZ—line 2) **b.** $ .00

**c.** Dividend income (IRS 1040 — line 9, or 1040A — line 9) **c.** $ .00

**d.** Net income (or loss) from business, farm, rents, royalties, partnerships, estates, trusts, etc. (IRS 1040 — lines 12, 18, and 19) If a loss, enter the amount in (parentheses). **d.** $ .00

**e.** Other taxable income such as alimony received, capital gains (or losses), pensions, annuities, etc. (IRS 1040—lines 10, 11, 13-15, 16b, 17b, 20, 21b, and 22, or 1040A—line 10) **e.** $ .00

**f.** Adjustments to income (IRS 1040 — line 30, or 1040A — line 12c) **f.** $ .00

**g.** Total (Add **73a-73e** minus **73f**.) **This is your answer to 24.** ——→ **g.** $ .00

**Section O — Divorced, Separated, or Remarried Parents**
(To be answered by the parent who completes this form, if the student's natural or adoptive parents are divorced or separated.)

**74. a.** Year of separation __ __ Year of divorce __ __

**b.** Other parent's name ______

Home address ______

Occupation/ Employer ______

**c.** According to court order, when will support for the student end? Month __ __ Year __ __

**d.** Who claimed the student as a tax exemption for 1989? ______

**e.** Is there an agreement specifying a contribution for the student's education? Yes ☐ 1 No ☐ 2

If yes, how much for the 1990-91 school year? $ .00

**Section P — Stafford (GSL) Loan Information** (Read the instructions on page 7.)

**75.** If it is necessary to borrow money to pay for educational expenses, do you want to be considered for a Stafford Loan? Yes ☐ 1 No ☐ 2

(If you marked "Yes," answer **76a-e**. Your information may be sent to the appropriate loan agency. If you marked "No," go to **77**. Skip **76**.)

**76.** Stafford (GSL) Loan information

**a.** Total unpaid balance on all your Stafford (GSL) Loans $ .00

**b.** Total unpaid balance on your most recent Stafford (GSL) Loan $ .00

**c.** Interest rate of your most recent Stafford (GSL) Loan (Mark only one box.) 1 ☐ 7% 2 ☐ 8% 3 ☐ 9% 4 ☐ 8/10%

**d.** Loan period of your most recent Stafford (GSL) Loan from __ __ Month __ __ Year through __ __ Month __ __ Year

**e.** Class level in which you received the most recent Stafford (GSL) Loan ☐ (Give number code from below.)

| | | |
|---|---|---|
| 1 = Freshman | 4 = Senior | 7 = Second year graduate/professional |
| 2 = Sophomore | 5 = Fifth year undergraduate | 8 = Third year graduate/professional |
| 3 = Junior | 6 = First year graduate/professional | 9 = Beyond third year graduate/professional |

**Section Q — Student's Colleges & Programs**

**77.** List the names and CSS code numbers of the colleges and programs to which you want CSS to send information from this form. Give the correct housing code. Don't list federal student aid programs. Be sure to include the college(s) you listed in **29**. Enclose the right fee. See the instructions and **78**.

| Name | City and State | CSS Code No. | Housing Code* |
|---|---|---|---|
| | | | |
| | | | |
| | | | |
| | | | |
| | | | |
| | | | |
| | | | |
| | | | |

***Housing Codes for 1990-91** (Enter only one code for each college.):
1 = With parents 2 = Campus housing 3 = Off-campus housing 4 = With relatives

**78. Fee:** Mark the box that tells how many colleges and programs are listed in **77**.

CSS Only

1 ☐ **$8.75** 3 ☐ **$22.25** 5 ☐ **$35.75** 7 ☐ **$49.25**
2 ☐ **$15.50** 4 ☐ **$29.00** 6 ☐ **$42.50** 8 ☐ **$56.00**

CSS Use Only

**Mail this form with a check or money order for the right amount made out to the College Scholarship Service. This form will be returned to you if no fee is enclosed.**

**Section R — Explanations/Special Circumstances**

CSS Use Only 1 5 6

Use this space to explain any unusual expenses, educational and other debts, or special circumstances.

# APPENDIX V
# SAMPLE WORKSHEET FOR THE PELL GRANT

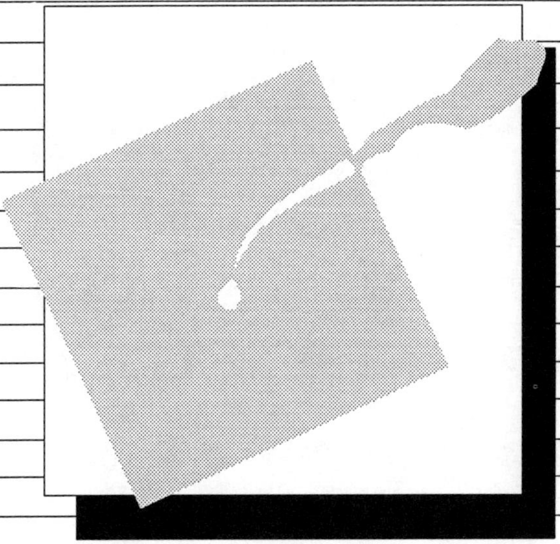

# SAMPLE WORKSHEET FOR THE PELL GRANT

## (DEPENDENT STUDENTS)

(reprinted from the PELL GRANT FORMULA,

1989-90, U.S. Department of Education)

***CASE STUDY 1 - JESSICA SWANLAKE (WISCONSIN)***

Jessica Swanlake, who is 22 years old and recently divorced, lives with her mother, who is also divorced. Jessica's younger brother is also a member of the household. Jessica's mother had an adjusted gross income of $12,500 in 1988, all of it earned from work. She also received $2,500 in child support, and paid $1,432 in Federal income tax. The family paid $600 in tuition and $200 for meals for the brother to attend a private elementary school. The family's house is worth $60,000, and there is a $20,000 mortgage against it. The family has a total of $500 in checking and savings accounts.

Jessica had $5,000 adjusted gross income in 1988, from her job as an office assistant, and paid $62 in Federal income tax. However, she was laid off when the factory closed, and is classified as a dislocated worker. On the date Jessica filed her student aid application she had $300 in savings. Jessica will be enrolled in a a two-year program at a community college. Because she will be taking a full course load, she only expects to earn $2,000 (with no income tax) in 1989, most of it working in the cafeteria over the summer. Her mother claimed her as an income tax exemption on her 1987 income tax return.

**NOTES TO CASE STUDY 1 - JESSICA SWANLAKE**

- ❑ As a single undergraduate student who was claimed by a parent as an income tax exemption, Jessica is considered dependent on her mother.
- ❑ Because Jessica and her mother had combined taxed income of $17,500, Jessica cannot use the simplified formula. However, she is considered a dislocated worker because she lost her job.
- ❑ The State tax allowance for Wisconsin is 12% for incomes of $15,000 or more.
- ❑ Only the tuition paid for Jessica's brother at the elementary school (not the cost of his meals) can be counted in the tuition offset.
- ❑ Because she is a dislocated worker, Jessica's income and U.S. taxes paid for 1988 are ignored. The $2,000 she expects to earn in 1989 is used instead, as well as her estimated taxes (0). Note that Jessica's status as a dislocated worker *does not* affect the calculation of the parental contribution -- her mother's 1988 income was used for that part of the calculation.

WORK SHEET **A**

# DEPENDENT STUDENT

**89-90 REGULAR FORMULA**

*Includes modifications for*
*-dislocated worker*
*-displaced homemaker*
*-special condition*

CASE STUDY #1 - Jessica Swanlake

## PARENTAL INCOME

| | |
|---|---|
| 1. 1988 TAXED INCOME (From IRS Form 1040-line 31, 1040A-line 13, 1040EZ-line 3. For non-tax filer, add 1A and 1B.) * | 12,500 |
| 1A. INCOME EARNED FROM WORK BY FATHER | |
| 1B. INCOME EARNED FROM WORK BY MOTHER | 12,500 |
| 2. 1988 UNTAXED INCOME AND BENEFITS (Social Security Benefits, AFDC, Child Support, Other.) * | 2,500 |
| 3. ONE-HALF OF STUDENT'S EXPECTED VETERANS EDUCATIONAL BENEFITS | 0 |
| 4. **TOTAL INCOME** (Lines 1 + 2 + 3) | 15,000 |
| 5. 1988 U.S. INCOME TAX PAID* | 1,432 |
| 6. STATE TAX ALLOWANCE (See Table 1) | 1,800 |
| 7. FAMILY SIZE OFFSET (See Table 2) | 8,400 |
| 8. MEDICAL/DENTAL OFFSET (Enter amount that **exceeds** 20% of: Total income minus U.S. and State taxes.) | 0 |
| 9. EMPLOYMENT EXPENSE OFFSET (Enter 50% of the lesser income from line 1A or 1B, not to exceed 1500.) | 1,500 |
| 10. TUITION OFFSET (Enter tuition paid — **not to exceed** total of 3750 times children for whom tuition is paid.) | 600 |
| 11. **TOTAL OFFSETS** (Add lines 5, 6, 7, 8, 9, 10) | 13,732 |
| 12. PARENTS' DISCRETIONARY INCOME (Line 4 minus line 11. If negative, enter as a negative number.) | 1,268 |
| ASSESSMENT RATE (See Table 3) | .11 |
| 13. **PARENTS' CONTRIBUTION FROM INCOME** (If negative, enter 0.) | 139 |

## PARENTAL ASSETS

| | |
|---|---|
| 14. NET VALUE OF HOME * (Home value minus home debt) | 40,000 |
| 14A. HOME ASSET RESERVE | - 30,000 |
| 14B. AVAILABLE HOME ASSETS (Line 14 minus reserve. If negative, enter 0.) | 10,000 |
| 15. NET VALUE OF OTHER ASSETS (Cash + checking + savings + real estate + investments minus real estate and investment debt.) | 500 |
| 15A. OTHER ASSETS RESERVE | - 25,000 |
| 15B. AVAILABLE OTHER ASSETS (Line 15 minus reserve. If negative, enter 0.) | 0 |
| 16. AVAILABLE FARM/BUSINESS ASSETS (Use Supplemental Worksheet.) | 0 |
| 17. TOTAL AVAILABLE PARENTAL ASSETS (Add lines 14B, 15B, and 16.) | 0 |
| 18. BASIC CONTRIBUTION FROM ASSETS (Multiply line 17 by .05. If result is negative, enter 0.) | 10,000 |
| 19. OFFSET FOR NEGATIVE DISCRETIONARY INCOME (If line 12 is negative, enter it as a positive number, otherwise enter 0.) | 500 |
| 20. **PARENTS' CONTRIBUTION FROM ASSETS** (Lines 18 - 19. If negative, enter as a positive number in 20A below, and enter 0 in box 20.) | 500 |
| 20A. | |
| 21. PARENTAL CONTRIBUTION FROM INCOME AND ASSETS (Lines 13 + 20.) | 639 |
| DIVIDE BY THE NUMBER OF FAMILY MEMBERS IN COLLEGE | 1 |
| 22. **TOTAL PARENTAL CONTRIBUTION** | 639 |

* Substitute 1989 expected taxed and untaxed income and use estimated U.S. taxes paid, if father or mother is a dislocated worker, or family qualifies for a special condition.

* Do not include home assets if father or mother is a dislocated worker or a displaced homemaker.

WORK SHEET A

# DEPENDENT STUDENT

*REGULAR FORMULA CONTINUED ...*

## STUDENT/SPOUSE INCOME

| | |
|---|---|
| *23.* 1988 TAXED INCOME (From IRS Form 1040-line 31, 1040A-line 13, 1040EZ-line 3. For non-tax filer, add 23A and 23B.) * | 2,000 |
| *23A.* INCOME EARNED FROM WORK BY STUDENT | 2,000 |
| *23B.* INCOME EARNED FROM WORK BY SPOUSE | |
| *24.* 1988 UNTAXED INCOME AND BENEFITS (Social Security Benefits, Other.) * | 0 |
| *25.* **TOTAL INCOME** (Lines 23 + 24.) | 2,000 |
| *26.* 1988 U.S. INCOME TAX PAID * | 0 |
| *27.* OFFSET FOR NEGATIVE INCOME (Enter amount from 20A, if any, as a positive number.) | 0 |
| *28.* OFFSET TO STUDENT INCOME (Single = $3600, Married = $5300) | 3,600 |
| *29.* **TOTAL OFFSETS** (Add lines 26, 27, and 28.) | 3,600 |
| *30.* STUDENT'S DISCRETIONARY INCOME (Line 25 minus line 29. If negative, enter 0.) | 0 |
| ASSESSMENT RATE | **X .75** |
| *31.* **STUDENT'S CONTRIBUTION FROM INCOME** | 0 |

## STUDENT/SPOUSE ASSETS

| | |
|---|---|
| *32.* NET VALUE OF HOME * (Home value minus home debt) | 0 |
| *33.* NET VALUE OF OTHER ASSETS (Cash + checking + savings + real estate + investments minus real estate and investment debt.) | 300 |
| *34.* NET FARM/BUSINESS ASSETS (F/B assets minus F/B debts.) | 0 |
| *35.* TOTAL AVAILABLE STUDENT/SPOUSE ASSETS (Add lines 32 + 33 + 34.) | 300 |
| ASSESSMENT RATE | **X .33** |
| *36.* **STUDENT'S CONTRIBUTION FROM ASSETS** | 99 |
| *37.* **STUDENT AID INDEX** (Add lines 22 + 31 + 36.) | 738 |

* Substitute 1989 expected taxed and untaxed income if student or spouse is a dislocated worker, and use estimated U.S. taxes paid.

* Do not include home assets if student or spouse is a dislocated worker or a displaced homemaker.

# APPENDIX VI

## ESTIMATING EXPECTED FAMILY CONTRIBUTION AND FINANCIAL NEED

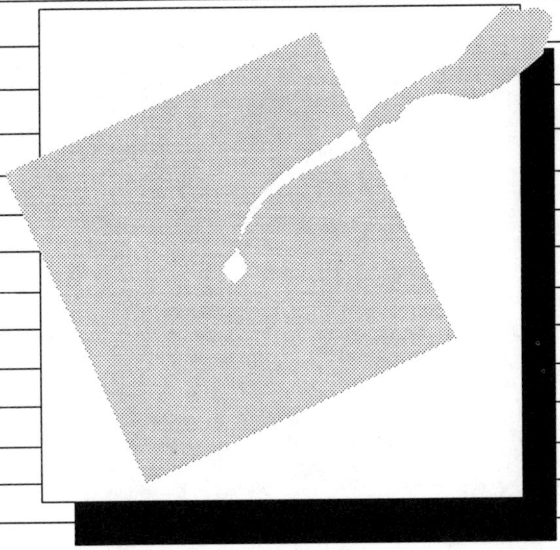

# ESTIMATING EXPECTED FAMILY CONTRIBUTION AND FINANCIAL NEED

# Estimating Expected Family Contribution and Financial Need—A Sample Case

The tables on the following page provide an estimate, based on average family circumstances, of what parents and students will be expected to contribute for a year of college education from their own resources. **Please keep in mind that these calculations only provide an approximation of what a family is expected to contribute for college expenses.** The official need analysis calculation will be determined by many factors, reflecting the financial circumstances of each family who applies. Students can find out their actual expected family contribution by requesting a copy of their need analysis when they file the 1991-92 ACT FFS or SAAC. You can request a copy of your need analysis in section P on the FFS or SAAC.

Table 2 on the following page shows how to estimate the amount Brenda Doyle and her family could contribute to her education and the amount of her financial need. Brenda comes from a family of five—her parents and three children. Of the three children, Brenda and one other will be in college. Brenda will be a freshman. Her older parent is 49.

First, Brenda's parents estimated their total income to be approximately $36,000 by combining their taxable and untaxed income and benefits.

Next, Brenda's parents estimated their total net assets to be approximately $60,000 by combining the value of their cash, savings and checking, home equity, and net worth of other real estate and investments.

To determine the estimated family contribution from Brenda's parents, refer to Table 1 under net assets of $60,000 for a family of five and total income of $36,000. As the table shows, the expected family contribution from Brenda's parents for family educational expenses equals $3,100.

Because there are two students in college, the family contribution is divided by two and Brenda's share from her parents will equal $1,550. As a first-year student, the minimum contribution Brenda is expected to make for her education is $700. Therefore, Brenda's estimated expected family contribution is ($1,550 + $700) $2,250.

Once an expected family contribution is calculated, that value is compared to the average costs of the college the student plans to attend. Brenda plans to attend a typical public college, which costs approximately $6,600. The difference between cost of education and the family contribution is called "financial need," or the amount of financial assistance the college will attempt to provide to students for one academic year. ☞

☞ In Brenda's case, her "financial need" is estimated to be $4,350.

If grants, loans, and scholarships are not enough to pay the entire bill for tuition and fees, the student will have to pay the balance from the expected family contribution. The rest of the expected family contribution will be spent as needed for books and supplies, rent, food, entertainment, transportation, personal expenses, etc.

Families should contact the financial aid office at the school their student plans to attend for more information about programs available at that institution.

# Estimating Expected Family Contribution and Financial Need

**TABLE 1**

ESTIMATED PARENTAL CONTRIBUTION AT VARIOUS INCOME, ASSET, AND FAMILY-SIZE LEVELS (August 1990)

| | SAVINGS AND OTHER ASSET EQUITY $20,000 | | | | $40,000 | | | | $60,000 | | | | $80,000 | | | |
|---|---|---|---|---|---|---|---|---|---|---|---|---|---|---|---|---|
| FAMILY SIZE | 3 | 4 | 5 | 6 | 3 | 4 | 5 | 6 | 3 | 4 | 5 | 6 | 3 | 4 | 5 | 6 |
| 1990 Earned Income | | | | | | | | | | | | | | | | |
| 8,000 | 0 | 0 | 0 | 0 | 0 | 0 | 0 | 0 | 0 | 0 | 0 | 0 | 100 | 0 | 0 | 0 |
| 12,000 | 0 | 0 | 0 | 0 | 0 | 0 | 0 | 0 | 300 | 0 | 0 | 0 | 800 | 200 | 0 | 0 |
| 16,000 | 0 | 0 | 0 | 0 | 400 | 0 | 0 | 0 | 900 | 300 | 0 | 0 | 1,400 | 900 | 300 | 0 |
| 20,000 | 700 | 100 | 0 | 0 | 1,000 | 400 | 0 | 0 | 1,500 | 900 | 400 | 0 | 2,000 | 1,500 | 1,000 | 400 |
| 24,000 | 1,300 | 700 | 200 | 0 | 1,600 | 1,000 | 500 | 0 | 2,100 | 1,600 | 1,000 | 400 | 2,800 | 2,100 | 1,600 | 1,000 |
| 28,000 | 2,000 | 1,400 | 800 | 200 | 2,200 | 1,600 | 1,100 | 500 | 2,900 | 2,200 | 1,600 | 1,100 | 3,600 | 2,800 | 2,200 | 1,600 |
| 32,000 | 2,700 | 2,000 | 1,500 | 800 | 3,000 | 2,300 | 1,700 | 1,100 | 3,800 | 2,900 | 2,300 | 1,700 | 4,700 | 3,700 | 3,000 | 2,200 |
| 36,000 | 3,600 | 2,800 | 2,100 | 1,500 | 3,900 | 3,100 | 2,400 | 1,700 | 4,900 | 3,900 | 3,100 | 2,300 | 6,000 | 4,800 | 3,900 | 3,000 |
| 40,000 | 4,700 | 3,700 | 2,900 | 2,200 | 5,100 | 4,000 | 3,200 | 2,400 | 6,200 | 5,000 | 4,000 | 3,100 | 7,300 | 6,100 | 5,000 | 3,900 |
| 44,000 | 6,000 | 4,800 | 3,900 | 2,900 | 6,400 | 5,200 | 4,200 | 3,200 | 7,500 | 6,300 | 5,200 | 4,000 | 8,600 | 7,400 | 6,300 | 5,000 |
| 48,000 | 7,100 | 6,000 | 5,000 | 3,900 | 7,400 | 6,400 | 5,400 | 4,200 | 8,500 | 7,500 | 6,500 | 5,200 | 9,700 | 8,600 | 7,600 | 6,400 |
| 52,000 | 8,200 | 7,100 | 6,100 | 5,000 | 8,500 | 7,400 | 6,500 | 5,300 | 9,600 | 8,600 | 7,600 | 6,400 | 10,800 | 9,700 | 8,700 | 7,600 |
| 56,000 | 9,400 | 8,300 | 7,300 | 6,200 | 9,700 | 8,600 | 7,700 | 6,500 | 10,800 | 9,800 | 8,800 | 7,600 | 12,000 | 10,900 | 9,900 | 8,800 |
| 60,000 | 10,600 | 9,500 | 8,500 | 7,400 | 10,900 | 9,800 | 8,900 | 7,700 | 12,000 | 11,000 | 10,000 | 8,800 | 13,200 | 12,100 | 11,100 | 10,000 |
| 64,000 | 11,800 | 10,700 | 9,700 | 8,600 | 12,100 | 11,100 | 10,100 | 8,900 | 13,200 | 12,200 | 11,200 | 10,100 | 14,400 | 13,300 | 12,300 | 11,200 |
| 68,000 | 13,000 | 11,900 | 10,900 | 9,800 | 13,300 | 12,300 | 11,300 | 10,100 | 14,400 | 13,400 | 12,400 | 11,300 | 15,600 | 14,500 | 13,500 | 12,400 |

The expected contribution figures above incorporate the following assumptions:

1. Two parents, one with income, all of which is taxable. Older parent is age 49. One child in college.
2. U.S. income taxes based on joint return and standard deduction. If income is $15,000 or less, Form 1040A filed.
3. No business or farm assets, unusual medical/dental expenses, or elementary/secondary tuition.
4. 1991-92 Congressional Methodology need analysis formula used for the estimates.

*Minimum student contribution for first-year students is $700. Minimum contribution for students beyond the first year is $900.

*Financial Need Worksheet Instructions*

*Step 1:*
Locate the proper Parental Contribution on Table 1 for your parents' income, net assets, and family size.

*Step 2:*
Divide the amount from Table 1 by the number of family members who will be in college and write the result on line 6 in Table 2.

*Step 3:*
Subtract lines 6 and 7 from line 5 and write the remainder on line 8. The remaining balance on line 8 (if any) is called "**financial need**" and is the amount the school will attempt to provide to the student from assorted types of financial aid which may consist of grants, loans, and/or work opportunities.

**TABLE 2**

**FINANCIAL NEED WORKSHEET**

| Budget Item | Brenda Doyle Typical Public College Costs | Typical Private College Costs | Your Choice |
|---|---|---|---|
| 1. Direct costs— Tuition & Fees | $ 2,000 | $ 8,000 | ______ |
| 2. Books & Supplies | 600 | 600 | ______ |
| 3. Indirect costs— Room & meals | 2,400 | 2,800 | ______ |
| 4. Miscellaneous— (personal, travel, recreation, clothes) | 1,600 | 1,600 | ______ |
| 5. TOTAL COSTS | 6,600 | 13,000 | ______ |
| 6. Minus Total Parental Contribution (from Table 1) | -1,550 | - ______ | - ______ |
| 7. Minus Average Student Contribution* | - 700 | - 700 | - 700 |
| 8. Remaining Balance (financial need) | $ 4,350 | $ ______ | $ ______ |

# FREE TO ALL PURCHASERS OF "THE MORE FOR YOUR MONEY GUIDES"

New and exciting free and deeply discounted offers are always being initiated and old ones rediscovered. To keep you informed and up-to-date on all the latest and best free offers and methods that you can take advantage of, we are offering all purchasers of our *More For Your Money Guides* a free issue of our "Best Things in Life for Free" newsletter.

Don't miss out on the newest and most innovative free opportunities available to you. Just send a self-addressed, stamped envelope to:

"Best Things in Life for Free"
P.O. Box 6661
Malibu, CA 90265

Some of the best things in life can be free! We are dedicated to providing the most fantastic, undiscovered and overloaded ideas and methods to obtain free goods, products and services for you and your family, and to alert you to the many opportunities to live, travel and enjoy life with little or no money. And, best of all, this information is free to our readers, just for asking.

Also perhaps you've also already had success with ideas of your own that have worked for you, that I haven't included in this book. If so, I would very much like to hear from you. Not only will sharing your ideas and successes be beneficial to others, but we will also pay $100 to the first person sending in an idea or method that we use in subsequent editions of our books, and $50 if it is used in our newsletter.